TALKING
TO LEARN

Talking
to learn

edited by

PAULINE JONES

PRIMARY ENGLISH TEACHING ASSOCIATION

National Library of Australia Cataloguing-in-Publication data

Talking to learn

Bibliography
ISBN 1 875622 19 5

1. Language arts (Primary).   2. Children – Language.
I. Jones, Pauline, 1958 – .   II. Primary English Teaching Association.

372.622

First published September 1996
Copyright © Primary English Teaching Association 1996
Laura Street Newtown NSW 2042 Australia
Cover illustration by Gary Bennell
Photographs by Damien Lee
Edited by Jeremy Steele
Designed by Anne-Marie Rahilly and Jeremy Steele
Formatted in 11/14 Janson by a.m. desktop
PO Box 95 Blaxland NSW 2774
Printed by Star Printery
21 Coulson Street Erskineville NSW 2043

Contents

Preface   vii

1   Language and learning   1
    PAULINE JONES

2   Planing an oral language program   11
    PAULINE JONES

3   Assessing oral language   27
    TINA SHARPE

4   Making the most of traditional newstime   44
    VICTORIA ROBERTS & VIVIENNE NICOLL

5   Newstime and oral narrative   54
    ROBYN CUSWORTH

6   Cooperative learning: enhancing talking and listening   66
    KATHY CREE & SANDRA DONALDSON

7   Towards meeting the needs of Aboriginal learners   80
    PENNI BRYDON, LESLEY MILLS & KATHLEEN RUSHTON

8   Talking to persuade: debating in the classroom   96
    VICKI POGULIS

9   Voice matters   114
    ISOBEL KIRK

10 Talk about literacy in the content areas   126
    PAULINE JONES

References   145

Notes on contributors   149

Acknowledgements

My thanks to those teachers in schools and elsewhere who have not only contributed their informed perspectives on and practices in oral language, but also participated in the project with such professionalism and generosity of spirit.

I am indebted to Viv Nicoll-Hatton for her thoughtful guidance and advice, to the PETA readers for their responses to the draft material, and to Dr Jeremy Steele for his editorial expertise and those patient lessons about writing and publishing.

An editor's job is never an easy one, but mine was made so much easier by the cooperation of those educators involved with specific target groups in our schools. I must thank Laurie Crawford, Aboriginal Teaching Fellow at Charles Sturt University, for his counsel and time given so generously. I am also fortunate to have had expert advice from Rob Healy of the NSW Aboriginal Education Consultative Group and Davina Tyrell, and I would like to thank the staff of the Disadvantaged Schools Centre, Metropolitan East Region, for their cooperation and response to materials.

Finally, I am grateful to Diana Pearce and Ellen Earley and the staff and students of Belmore South Public School and Camdenville Public School for assisting us, despite the myriad demands of busy schools, to collect such wonderful images of children talking and listening.

Preface

Several themes emerge from this book, and the first is embedded in its title *Talking To Learn*. Children spend a number of years learning to talk and using talk to learn about their social and cultural worlds. As teachers we need to acknowledge what these young learners can already do with and through talk, as well as recognising the centrality of talk throughout primary school learning.

A further theme running through the book is the diversity of background among learners in our classrooms. There are large variations in children's experiences of the world and their ways of looking at it, with consequent differences in their spoken language repertoires. Thus the teachers who write here, all of whom are considered outstanding practitioners, describe experiences with many different groups. Yet their writings convey a common respect, care and admiration for their students. They also share a concern for making aspects of language visible for all learners — a 'taught rather than caught' approach.

Assessing and planning are mutually informing activities; hence the decision to locate Tina Sharpe's chapter on assessment towards the beginning of the book. Too often assessment is left until last, appearing almost as an afterthought. However, assessing oral language gives teachers valuable evidence on which to base judgements about children's learning, as well as their social and language development. Subsequent chapters describe the teaching and learning (and therefore assessing) opportunities in these areas.

A final theme of the book is collaboration. Good teaching is a shared endeavour, between teachers, between teacher and students, and between students and students. Much of the material in the book is the result of teachers' collaborative activity. Teachers talk to each other as they plan for learning and record their intentions. They talk while they teach, and while they reflect on their actions and those of their learners. In writing here, these particular teachers are extending the dialogue about spoken language in the classroom.

1

Language and learning

P A U L I N E   J O N E S

Early language and learning

The oral language that children bring to school is a remarkably rich resource — one which provides them with the means of negotiating their worlds. Let's begin, then, by looking at an example of a younger child developing this resource. Dominic is two and a half years old and bilingual, growing up speaking Spanish and English. In the following transcript he is looking at books with his father, Ramon, and mother, Criss.

R:	*(picking up 'Imagine')* Vamos a leer este.	Let's read this.
D:	*(bringing another book)* Vamos leer este.	Let's read this.
C:	En espanol con Pape.	In Spanish with Daddy.
D:	Este libro is Pape's.	This book is Daddy's.
C:	Con Pape.	With Daddy.
D:	Look at this! . . . I . . . I . . . Imagine . . . I . . . Little little one. *(taking the book from R)* I this back.	
R:	Esta bien . . . Como?	Good . . . What?
	Quiere leer en espanol?	Do you want to read it in Spanish?
	Voy a ponerlo atras . . . pon lo atras.	I'll put it behind . . . put it behind.
D:	Snake . . .	
R	*(starts reading the text in Spanish)* A ver . . . Imaginate . . .	Let's see . . . Imagine . . .
D:	Snake . . .	
R:	Si vies los pajaros?	Do you see the birds?

Como se dice una snake en espanol,	How do you say snake in Spanish,
como se dice?	how do you say it?
(waiting for D) Snake se dice . . . serpiente.	Snake says . . . snake.
D: Serpiente.	Snake.
R: Como se dice . . . serpiente?	How do you say . . . snake?
Vamos a buscar una . . . serpiente, no?	Let's look for a . . . snake, no?

Dominic is learning language by building up speaking and listening skills — in his case, in two languages. These languages enable him (with the help of others close to him) to develop understandings that include the literacy practices of his home and community.

Another child, Ellen, monolingual and two years older than Dominic, demonstrates how oral language allows her to take steps towards understanding what she observes. After witnessing a change in scene and time during a television show, she asks:

E: Hey Mum! You know in that story 'Cinderella'? How come it goes ball – boom – wedding – ball – boom – wedding?

M: Oh well, that's the tricks of movie makers and writers. They make time seem to go much faster than it really does.

In the normal course of events the adults about Ellen would probably not initiate a discussion about time and relativity, but this dialogue indicates the way in which spoken language enables her to gain some control over ideas she needs to pursue. She was to return to the topic twice in subsequent days: once to point out what she felt was a more realistic representation of time in a different version of the fairy tale which interposed some activity between the ball and the wedding; once to introduce a scene change indicating the passage of time in dramatic play with her brother.

Through their interactions with others in the years prior to school, Dominic and Ellen have built up their own stores of social and cultural knowledge. Oral language has been a powerful tool in this development and will continue to be crucial for both of them at school, where it will become the key to specialised subject areas and lead to consciously literate modes of language use. It will also be the means through which they broaden their social relationships to include their peer group and adults outside home and close community environments.

Oral language and the curriculum

English is unique as a learning area in that it is both a subject in its own right and the major vehicle for learning in other subject areas. Spoken and written English are accorded equal status in current curriculum documents, which

A young student relates an incident to her older friends during lunchtime. Buddy systems and peer support programs not only help to develop a sense of community among students of different ages, but also broaden the range of opportunities for informal language use.

describe texts broadly as spoken, written or visual (as in posters and public signs), or as combinations of these (as in picture books, film and CD-ROM encyclopaedias). Spoken texts include conversations, speeches, advertisements, broadcast programs and dramatic performances, and will be drawn from literature, specialised subject areas, everyday texts and the media.

In producing and interpreting spoken texts, language users draw on knowledge of their social and cultural worlds (i.e. *contextual understandings*) and the skills involved in segmenting streams of sound into words and sentences (i.e. *knowledge of linguistic structures and features*). Contextual understandings refer to our awareness of how the context in which a text is produced affects the language used. They can be considered from two points of view, the first of which is concerned with the broad level of culture.

The *context of culture* influences speakers and listeners in ways which include:

- appropriateness (what it is considered appropriate to talk about, with whom and where)

- genre (the ways in which certain social activities are negotiated, such as storytelling, shopping, job interviews or small talk).

Variations in these two factors reflect what different groups of language users have come to value. For example, Standard Australian English, the language of public institutions like school, is but one of the many varieties of English which make up Australian English. Genres also vary — what is judged appropriate in one cultural context may not be so in another. The result is that the context of culture is not singular but diverse. Effective communicators are aware of this and are constantly negotiating meaning across the differences.

Individuals will interpret and produce texts according to multiple influences: for instance, age, gender, religious beliefs, ethnicity, geographical location and personal experience. Examples of varying interpretations can often be heard in the range of comments made by movie goers leaving the cinema. Students need to be aware of these variable factors and become skilled at interpreting and constructing texts in different cultural contexts.

The second point of view from which to consider context is concerned with situational knowledge — what is called the *context of situation*. In any particular situation the purpose of an interaction will be a major influence on the language used. Purposes demanded by the curriculum and school life include informing, instructing, entertaining, describing and persuading. Skilled speakers and listeners can vary their choice of language according to:

- *the role that spoken language is playing in the interaction* (e.g. the language used to explain and play a board game is different from that used to tell an amusing anecdote)
- *the topic or activity* being spoken about
- *the roles and relationships* between the speakers, or between speaker and audience.

Together these factors determine the *register* of a text. Students have to develop the linguistic resources required to engage with a variety of registers — that is, texts produced in the many different formal and informal, social and educational situations they will encounter over time.

Contextual factors, both cultural and situational, are embedded in or realised through the *linguistic structures and features* of texts. These include:

- the structure of texts (e.g. orientation, series of events, reorientation is a typical structure of recounts)
- text cohesion, or the way a text 'hangs together'
- grammar and vocabulary choices, determined largely by the topic.

Spoken texts also draw on aspects of phonology and paralinguistic features. Speakers and listeners rely on sounds, intonation patterns and rhythm to exchange meaning. Pitch, pause, emphasis and stress figure in this process, and body language, such as gesture, facial expression and posture, is also important.

In short, school makes new demands on children in terms of spoken language use. As the contexts for language broaden, Ellen and Dominic will encounter different ways of making meaning. These differences can be considered in terms of the three register components: field, tenor and mode.

Field: Children are expected to participate in spoken language activities centred on various curriculum topics (such as rainforests or three-dimensional shapes), on social relationships (such as peer support activities), and on learning itself (through such strategies as self-reflection and evaluation). Topics for talk will progress from the familiar to the abstract. This learning progression requires access to specialised vocabulary, to expressions of thinking such as cause-effect and contrastive relationships, to ways of clarifying or checking understandings, and to the kind of language used to discuss language and literacy (i.e. a *metalanguage*).

Tenor: The higher child-to-adult ratio encountered at school represents a major shift from the more intimate relationships formed between children and their caregivers and siblings in the pre-school years. Learning to be a member of a large group will be a fresh challenge for most children and one they cannot avoid, for the group in various guises is the dominant organisational form for instruction and disseminating information inside and outside the classroom.

For some, school will present the first experience of collaborative tasks with other children. This change places new demands on children's language for negotiation. Interpersonal skills and the concomitant language resources not only shape playground experiences for individuals but, because of the emphasis on group work in many primary classrooms, will to some extent determine their level of success in learning.

Mode: Children engage in spoken language activities which range from familiar context-embedded activities (such as building with construction blocks or commenting on a sequence of pictures) to tasks requiring more reflective uses of language, in which aspects of audience, purpose and form are emphasised (e.g. formal debates and spoken reports).

Kindergarten teachers, recognising the challenge of these demands for young learners, often employ strategies which minimise the novelty of some aspects of register. They will use familiar topics related to self, family and community on which to build experience in the early weeks while children adjust to school life.

Learner diversity and needs

Effective teaching is based on what children already know and can do. The teaching of English will achieve most where the considerable informal language knowledge and competence of students, whatever their cultural or language backgrounds, is acknowledged, used and extended.

(Curriculum Corporation 1994, p. 5)

Children beginning school will already have had experience of using oral language for a range of purposes — experience which will help to shape their performance at school. For example, Ellen has spent a good deal of time with her father, a gardener, and has helped to establish a flourishing vegetable garden. In the following transcript she is working with her mother, whom she senses is less confident in the garden; she adjusts her language accordingly. (Mother and daughter were taking lettuce seedlings from a punnet and planting them.)

> E: Push it out like that.
>   Careful of those little roots . . .
>   Well now . . .
>   Now, I'll give you the seed.
>   You put . . . oh!
>   Here's yours.
>   Now, here, you hold up the leave (*sic*) and I'll bury it around . . .
>   This got two plants in it!

Ellen's knowledge of the plant world and its associated vocabulary (and her skills in using the instruction genre) should serve her well in the fields of science and literacy, providing that she is supported in the move into more specialised understandings. Outside school, however, children will have very different experiences of the fields and tenor relationships associated with school and the uses for which language is employed there. So, just as school signals register demands different from those of the pre-school years, it also demands different things of different children.

Dominic and Ellen both have mothers engaged in the field of education and have spent several years in organised child care. Consequently they will come to school familiar with Standard Australian English, the language of instruction. However, considerable numbers of children will encounter this school variety of English for the first time. Prominent among those emerging with specific needs in oral language programs will be Aboriginal and Torres Strait Islander children and ESL learners (of course there may be some overlap between these groups).

Teachers need to become aware of some of the issues arising from the language practices of Aboriginal and Torres Strait Islander communities. For many speakers of Kriol or Torres Strait Creole, English is a foreign language. Other children speak variants of Standard Australian English at home and in the community. These variants are not 'incorrect'; rather they are legitimate languages and dialects which 'reflect, maintain and continually create Aboriginal culture and identity' (DEET 1995, p. 12). The task for the teacher is to support continued development of home languages and dialects, while demonstrating the purposes and contexts for which Standard Australian English is appropriate and helping students to develop their skills in using it.

The needs of children for whom English is not a first language

Children from homes where a language other than English is spoken comprise almost one quarter of the school population (Gibbons 1992, p. 225). Some, like Dominic, will have been born in Australia and begin school bilingual. Others born in Australia will begin school fluent in a language or languages other than English, and may or may not have developed literacy skills in them. Still others will have been born overseas and arrive in Australian schools at various entry points. These students may be bilingual (in the sense of fluency in both languages) and will certainly have differing literacy skills. Some will have been through severe traumas, such as family breakup, war or famine, and have had either little or severely disrupted schooling. For many, the process of family migration and settlement will have been unsettling in itself.

Newly arrived students are the most visible of the group who are learning English as a second language. They must have ready access to specialist teachers, but they are not normally segregated from the mainstream classroom, since this is seen as a critical site for social and educational development, and therefore for language development. There are several factors mainstream teachers can usefully consider when they are planning oral language programs for a class which includes a newly arrived child:

- Expect a 'silent period' during which the student will concentrate on using all of his or her available resources to understand and participate in the new environment. In other words, he or she will be focusing on the receptive skills of listening, watching and reading rather than the productive skills of speaking and writing.

- Encourage use of the student's first language, whether through opportunities to work with another native speaker of the same language (e.g. a peer, an older student or a community member) or the use of bilingual tapes and books. This not only assists ongoing conceptual development, but also sends a clear message to the newly arrived student that home languages are valued in the school environment.

- Design and adapt learning experiences that enable the newly arrived student to work on the same content as and with other class members. This may involve the use of a range of contextual supports, such as diagrams, charts, pictures and artefacts. Although newly arrived students will be working toward different outcomes initially, they need access to the mainstream curriculum.

- Monitor teacher talk to avoid confusing the student with ambiguity and colloquialisms. Try particularly to be consistent in signals for routine events and instructions during this initial period.

Because access to the mainstream curriculum is seen as a priority for ESL students and it is usual practice to place them in mainstream classes, a large number are to be found there. Yet while some of them enjoy success, a good many others do not achieve as highly as their native-speaking peers. Frequently they receive inadequate support in class because they do not stand out as ESL learners, being Australian-born and having enough English to successfully negotiate social life inside and outside the classroom.

Cummins and Swain (1986) have described the difference between the language demands of the playground and daily routines and those of specialised curriculum areas. (Playground and routine language is also known as basic interpersonal skills competency [BISC], in contrast to cognitive academic language proficiency [CALP].) Face-to-face interpersonal language skills are relatively easy to pick up, but the conceptually related language skills take ESL learners considerably longer to acquire. In many cases their competency in social English distracts attention from their needs in terms of decontextualised academic language. However, like all learners, they need to be competent in both types of language.

Effective teaching strategies for academic and social language competence are based on the following tenets.

Language development is driven by purposeful language use.

Students need plenty of varied opportunities for language use. In the primary school language use is related to social and curriculum purposes, and students need to be involved in motivating learning experiences which are both linguistically and cognitively challenging. For example, consider the following problem-solving task included in a unit of work about animals:

With a partner, select a zoo animal. Design and make a model of an enclosure for a group of those animals. Your enclosure should reflect the animal's natural environment and allow for its behaviours.

Such tasks require learners to use language associated with the topic (e.g. *zoo, enclosure, giraffes, elephants, habitat, diet*) and with problem solving (e.g. *If . . . , then . . . It has to have . . .*), as well as with collaboration (e.g. *I think . . . What about . . . ? Yes/No, because . . .*). At the same time as their language skills are being stretched, learners are required to demonstrate their understandings of animal characteristics and needs, zoo facilities and design, and construction techniques.

Language is shaped by the social and cultural contexts in which it is produced.
Second language learners need classroom practices which make the links between texts and contexts explicit. They include:

- interrogating the social purpose (e.g. *Who is the speaker? Who is the intended audience? What is the speaker trying to do? How else might it be done? What is your response? Where else do we find this type of talk?*)

- modelling examples of the genre through role play or audio and video tape, or through deconstructing texts (e.g. *What sort of shape is this text? What function does this part have? How does the text hang together? How effective is it?*)

Over time students and teachers build up a good deal of technical language with which to talk about their shared understandings. Classrooms which enable students to develop the tools for thinking and talking about language and the construction of texts serve ESL students particularly well.

Bilingualism and biculturalism are strengths.
Students' prior experiences of learning language and culture are a resource which they can draw on in learning a second or subsequent language and culture. For example, most ESL learners who are already literate in another language do not have to relearn concepts about print in order to read and write in English. Likewise those who have developed understandings about the world in their first language can readily transfer them to their second; they don't need to learn them again. In addition, the process of learning a second language helps students to develop considerable metalinguistic awareness, and as a result ESL learners tend to be comfortable with explicit talk about language forms and practices.

Practices which value children's linguistic and cultural resources can have a powerful effect on their self-esteem. For example, a classroom using culturally significant motifs and artefacts to help students explore

It's natural for these girls to use their first language rather than Standard Australian English as they check homework. Many bilingual and bidialectal speakers move easily between situations demanding different things of their language skills.

mathematical concepts can make strong links between home and school and reinforce cultural identity in a positive way. Programs which explore the many ways of meeting social needs (e.g. greeting and leave taking, performing family duties, recording important information, or celebrating) help all children to build up a framework for understanding and valuing the language and culture of their own communities as well as of others.

Conclusion

This chapter has stressed the important role of spoken language in learning, while attempting to describe some of the diverse aspects of the language in use among learners in our mainstream classes. The current curriculum guidelines which consider language in relation to the context in which it's produced strongly support the needs of all learners, and the following chapter draws on them to consider certain implications for classroom practice.

Acknowledgement
Many thanks to Criss Jones Diaz for the use of a transcript of her family life.

2

Planning an oral language program

PAULINE JONES

The nature of spoken language

One of the difficulties of considering oral language in the classroom is that spoken forms of language are much more difficult to capture than written forms. Most spoken language is dialogic: that is, constructed by two or more people. As a result it is often fragmented and hard to predict as speakers and listeners interact to request or clarify details, monitor actions, change topic, agree or disagree. Several of these features are evident in an extended transcript of the gardening activity from the previous chapter.

> E: Push it out like that.
> Careful of those little roots!
> Well now . . .
> Now, I'll give you the seed.
> You put . . . oh!
> Here's yours.
> Now, here, you hold up the leave (*sic*) and I'll bury it around . . .
> This got two plants in it!
> M: It has.
> Do we put them both in?
> I guess we do.
> That's little, isn't it?
> E: *(nods)* Now, my one . . . too deep.
> M: No, that's alright.

Ellen's mother follows her daughter's instructions, agrees with the observation about two seedlings rather than one and wonders what to do about it. Ellen's next conversational move is to monitor her mother's planting technique (*too deep*) but her mother demurs. Such intricacy is typical of much of the language produced in face-to-face interactions. The question *That's little, isn't it?* doesn't even draw a verbal reply — Ellen's nod is sufficient response.

Speaking and listening tend to happen in the same place, in a shared context, and gesture, facial expression and objects in the immediate vicinity are all available to aid communication. By contrast, written language is usually monologic and composed at a location and time different from those of the reader. Look, for instance, at the printed set of instructions which accompanied the seedlings:

> *First water the punnet, then carefully place the seedlings upside down on your hand and remove punnet. Keep as much soil on roots as possible when planting. Firm seedlings into soil, keep crown of seedling above soil level.*

In speaking Ellen was able to refer to items in the immediate context by using *that, those* and *it*. However, the written instructions are more specific, and items like *seedlings, punnet, crown* and *soil* are named. Writers cannot draw on support from a shared context and so must recreate the context for the reader. They must be more explicit about the manner in which actions take place: for example, *carefully place, upside down, as much . . . as possible, keep crown of seedling above . . .* Using lexical items (or naming words) is one way in which writers pack information in. Hence written language is typically said to be more lexically dense than spoken language.

Oral and written language: two ways of knowing

Spoken and written language are used for different purposes. In speaking and listening we tend to be getting something done, exploring ideas, working out some aspect of the world or simply being together. In writing we may be creating a record, committing events or moments to paper. When Ellen recounted the lettuce planting for an adult to scribe onto a postcard to her grandmother that evening, she interpreted the experience in a very different way:

> *Dear Grandma,*
> *There's a big Christmas tree of lettuce. We planted new lettuce and I think they are going to grow up like that tall Christmas tree of lettuce and I want to use that tall lettuce next Christmas for a tree.*
> > *Love from Ellen*
> *(Dad says the tall lettuce is too old.)*

During planting Ellen was concerned with the action or process of getting the lettuce into the ground (*give, put, bury, hold*), while her concern in the recounted version shifts to the plants themselves (*new lettuce, tall Christmas tree of lettuce*). Halliday (1985, p. 97) describes spoken and written language as 'two grids on experience': spoken language is essentially dynamic, about happenings, while written language is synoptic, about things.

Teachers usually recognise the importance of these differences and plan curriculum units in which the focus varies between spoken and written language. Because of the critical role of spoken language in learning, speaking activities tend to precede writing activities, helping students to build the necessary background knowledge demanded by reading and writing across curriculum areas.

However, there isn't always a clear dividing line between spoken and written language, inside or outside the classroom. Because of this, the notion of mode is useful for considering spoken language tasks, and in particular the action-reflection continuum.

informal face-to-face chat	small group problem-solving tasks	reporting back on a task	newstime	spoken information reports	reading aloud

---

most spoken-like   **most written-like**

language accompanying action	class discussions	show and tell			language as reflection

(adapted from Martin 1985)

FIG. 2.1. THE MODE CONTINUUM

The texts from either pole of the continuum reveal the most distinct differences between spoken and written language. It's easy to describe the spoken lettuce-planting text, with its dependence on the immediate context, as language accompanying action. It would be positioned close to the most spoken-like end of the continuum. Ellen's recount to her grandmother is typical of much informal writing in that reads rather like speech written down. It would be positioned further along the continuum towards written-like texts, although it still shares some characteristics with speech.

Other oral language activities typically found in classrooms may be positioned according to factors such as predictability, the possibility of interruption or interaction, and dependence on contextual support. Many oral activities share features of the written mode and hence fall further along the continuum. Tasks such as reporting on an activity or presenting an oral argument tend to be monologic and have recognisable structures and grammatical features in common with written texts.

Talk as process and performance

In planning for oral language it's helpful to consider talk in two categories: *talk as process* and *talk as performance*. Examples are given in the lists below.

Talk as process	Talk as performance
collaborative problem solving	morning news
joint text constructions	sports reports
class discussions	debating
individual writing conferences	joke telling, anecdotes
brainstorming, listing	dramatic presentations
giving directions, instructions	retelling
construction activities	storytelling
board games	delivering oral messages
writers/readers circles	thanking a guest speaker

Talk as process refers to learning experiences in which talk is associated with other activities. For example, students may be engaged in hands-on activities to explore concepts associated with floating and sinking. In this type of spoken language students and teachers usually focus on meaning or on talking their way to understanding. Such talk will be clustered around the most spoken-like end of the continuum.

Talk as performance refers to spoken language activities that take account of an audience. Like written tasks, these formal spoken tasks (such as information reports and morning news) often have identifiable generic structures and the language used is more predictable. The resulting texts will be positioned towards the most written-like end of the continuum. Because of less contextual support, the speaker must include all necessary information in the text — hence the importance of topic as well as textual knowledge. And while meaning is still important, there will be more emphasis on form and accuracy. Effective class programs should contain a balance of both performance and process talk so that students encounter a realistic range of spoken texts.

Routine opportunities for talk

The spontaneous nature of talk means that it's impossible to plan for every spoken language encounter. For example, the immediate social and physical environments of the classroom account for a good deal of routine talk — morning greetings, instructions, and interactions with a number of different adults, including parent helpers, relief and specialist teachers, non-teaching staff and visitors.

A genuine interest in communication expressed in routine encounters does much to build individual self-esteem, as well as class cohesion. The

Talk as process — talking is just as vital in jointly constructing a house as it is in the joint construction of text.

Talk as performance — this student is rehearsing the retelling of a story. Her audience is prepared to offer advice about delivery as well as content.

relationships between students and teachers owe much to shared knowledge of aspects of each other's lives (e.g. pets, family members, friends and interests), and this comparative intimacy is built up through regular classroom talk, which won't always be in Standard English. However, there are inevitably misunderstandings or mishaps within the routine of classroom life, and students may need to work through appropriate responses to situations like these:

What might you say when —
- *someone says something that hurts your feelings?*
- *you accidentally spill glue on someone else's book?*
- *someone collects your lunch from the canteen and begins to eat it?*
- *you have to return a damaged book to the library?*

The communicative classroom

Whether talk is routine or planned, there are some important factors to consider in fostering genuine communication in classrooms.

Making the rules visible

Classrooms in which interaction is encouraged are likely to be fertile sites for successful oral language programs. Oral language flourishes particularly in classrooms where small groups are routinely formed. In all classrooms, however, there will be moments of teacher direction as teaching points or organisational issues are dealt with, and it's important to have clear and shared ideas of expected behaviours, just as it is to have procedures in place for solving problems and resolving disputes.

In communicative classrooms students and teachers frequently discuss and isolate factors that make good talkers and listeners. Many teachers record and display them as a reminder (see Fig. 2.2 for an example). Such discussions can lead to an exploration of cultural differences (e.g. eye contact) and contextual differences (e.g. the expectations of good listeners and talkers in a partner activity as compared with a whole class discussion).

Teachers also need to continually provide models of good spoken language and the processes of active listening. One I know recommends a listening time after a teacher joins a group before he or she says anything.

Classroom organisation

The physical organisation and layout of the classroom can have quite an effect on opportunities for interaction. Best is the kind of layout that enables students to move quickly and easily between whole class, small group, pair

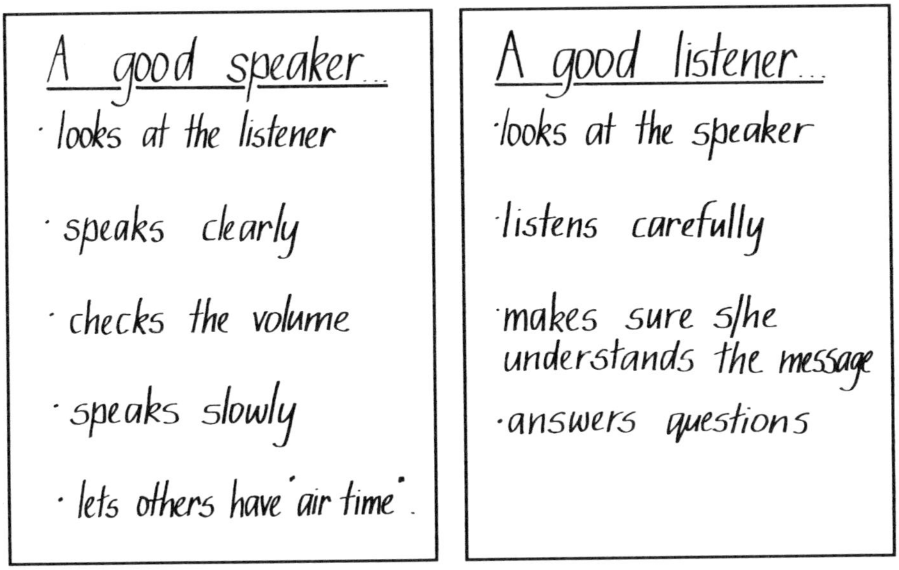

<u>A good speaker</u>...
- looks at the listener
- speaks clearly
- checks the volume
- speaks slowly
- lets others have "air time".

<u>A good listener</u>...
- looks at the speaker
- listens carefully
- makes sure s/he understands the message
- answers questions

FIG. 2.2. WALL CHARTS

and individual activities. Interest corners, learning centres, quiet listening spaces, and construction, preparation and performance areas are all desirable for listening and speaking activities, while younger students should have access to space and materials for dramatic play. Students also need to be able to locate (and care for) resources independently.

Broader audiences

The daily lives of schools give rise to quite a variety of opportunities for using spoken language — communicating messages from classroom to classroom, participating in the school council, escorting visitors, using telephones, giving instructions and recounting events. From time to time students are also required to prepare public texts for thanking guest speakers or for delivery at special events, ceremonies and so on. Often such activities fall outside the scope of specific units of work, and yet students still need to know the appropriate conventions. Teachers can give them support through modelling and by allowing them extended time to rehearse. This support should be built into the oral language program.

Designing activities for talk as performance

Initially talk as performance needs to be prepared for and scaffolded in much the same way as written text, and many of the teaching strategies used to make understandings of written text accessible can be applied to the more formal uses of spoken language. For instance, models can be supplied from video or audio recordings, transcripts, written dialogues or role plays. They may be authentic or specially constructed. Popular genre-based teaching practices like the ones described below can be used to structure activities.

Deconstruction

It's possible to explore the social context of a text with questions like these:

> *What's the purpose of this text? What's it trying to do? What's it about? Who is/are the speaker/s? Who's the intended audience?*

Text deconstruction activities which enable students and teachers to consider genre and language features are also useful. Guiding questions might include:

> *What shape or structure does this text have? What does each part do? What sort of language is found in each part? What words related to the topic are used? What sort of relationship is there between the speaker and the listener or audience?*

The resulting understandings about context and genre features can be drawn on during joint construction of another model.

The use of supports like palm cards, diagrams or posters might also be a part of modelling. The set of palm cards reproduced in Fig. 2.3 were used by a young child during a spoken information report on spiders, the pictures serving as prompts.

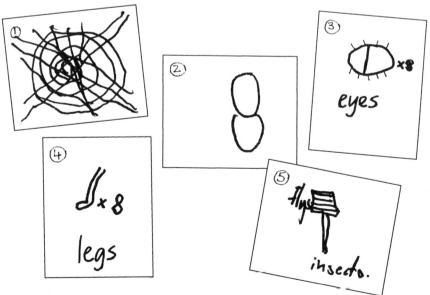

FIG. 2.3. PALM CARDS

Joint construction

Learning to construct and deliver more formal spoken texts involves recognising the importance of planning. The amount needed varies of course; some tasks require students merely to think through or mentally rehearse the parts of a message, while others involve quite extensive preparation. For example, spoken information reports require students to research and organise material in much the same way as they would in preparing a written report.

The planning and research process needs to be modelled clearly for students while they are gaining control over these types of spoken text. In joint construction teacher and students will be attending both to content and form, perhaps using questions like these:

> *What do we want to say?*
> *Why are we saying it?*
> *To whom?*
> *Where else do we find this type of talk?*
> *How might we say it? What shape might it have?*
> *What words will we need? Let's write them on cards to help us remember.*

After considering such questions, joint construction can begin — *Who would like to start the talk?* The completed text might be taped and then replayed for collaborative reviews. A further joint construction would demonstrate the importance of rehearsing such texts.

Individual construction

Many tasks like delivering classroom messages or buying lunch require brief modelling before younger students can be expected to perform them independently, though with a little planning or rehearsal they become habitual. However, students will benefit from being able to rehearse more extended tasks onto tape or to a supportive audience, so that they can reflect and adjust their material and delivery to suit their final audience.

Designing activities for talk as process

Second language teaching, with its emphasis on language in use, cognitive as well as linguistic challenge, and participation for all students, can provide some useful activities for adaptation to mainstream classrooms. These include information gap activities, role plays and problem-solving tasks, all of which are described below. Including such activities in a curriculum program can enhance the oral language development of all students.

Information gap activities

There are a number of types of information gap activities. They are usually pair or small group tasks, based on distributing information among pairs or small groups of students so that each one has a different share (or sometimes none). It's essential that no student can see the information distributed to another, and so some teachers erect a physical barrier like an open book or folder between participants (hence the term *barrier games*), while others have them sit back-to-back. The students then work together, using language only to reconstruct the information or otherwise complete the task. Some different types of information gap activities are described below.

Communicative crosswords. A has all the horizontal answers and B has the corresponding set of vertical answers. A nominates a blank space (e.g. *1 down*) and B, who knows the word that fits there, responds by devising a clue like a definition or a phonic hint (e.g. *it's used for fishing* or *it rhymes with book*). A then tries to identify the word and B confirms it or continues to supply clues until A is successful. B then nominates a blank space (e.g. *2 across*) and A supplies a clue. The game continues like this until both students have completed crosswords.

Describe and make/draw tasks. A has a completed picture or model and gives B instructions for drawing or making an identical one. Emphasis can be on both students contributing information to successfully complete the task: that is, A gives directions but B can ask questions to clarify details. Tangrams, beads or construction blocks can also be used in these tasks.

Same or different/Find the difference. A and B are given pictures with slightly different details. They describe their pictures to each other and try to identify the differences.

Complete the map. A and B are given plans of the same area with different features shown on each. They must work together to add all the features to both maps. (Coordinates are a great help here.)

Information transfer. Students are given identical diagrams, but A has diagram and labels, while B has diagram and captions. Together they label and caption both diagrams.

Split stories/sentences. This is a group activity which requires the teacher to select several short texts and divide them into portions. Students are each given a strip of paper with a portion of text, which they memorise. They then try to locate the students with the remainder of their text and together try to sequence and retell it.

Role plays

Role plays can be used in a number of curriculum contexts. The framework given to students can vary from just the scene and characters to one containing a good deal more detail. Role plays provide students with opportunities to extend their language repertoires by increasing the number of situations (and therefore registers) available in the classroom. They're a useful way of exploring community issues too: for example, role plays centred on woodchipping allow students to consider the points of view of environmentalists, timber workers and politicians.

Students may need some kind of introduction to role plays. For younger children this can take the form of dramatic play around familiar activities like shopping; they might each be given a picture of the person they have to 'be'. Older students may benefit from the 'Say-It' exercise, which involves them working in pairs with a grid like the one shown in Fig. 2.4. When A calls out a square (e.g. *1a*), B must do what is described in that square.

1a	2a	3a
Pretend that this is your first day at a new school. Say your name. Say where you come from.	*The principal asks you about your hobbies.* Tell her about three things you enjoy doing in your spare time.	*You are going to buy your lunch.* Ask how much it costs. Ask and pay for the things you want.
1b	2b	3b
Compare your last year's class with this one. Describe two differences.	*Invite a friend to your house after school.* Say why you want her or him to come.	*You have to go and see the school assistant.* Ask a friend how to get there.
1c	2c	3c
You are sitting next to a new friend. Ask him or her to help you with a spelling problem.	*Your school wants to raise some money for buying library books.* Give two ideas for raising the money.	*You have just got home from school.* Tell a parent what you did at school. Tell about two things you saw on the way home.

(adapted from Nation and Thomas 1988, p. 22)

FIG. 2.4. EXAMPLE OF THE 'SAY-IT' EXERCISE

'Hot Seat' is a form of role play which gives students the opportunity to imagine themselves to be someone else and consider motivation for actions. One student is given the role of a real or imaginary character (e.g. a sports star or other well-known person, or a character from a shared narrative) and occupies the hot seat. Others adopt questioning roles to explore what motivates the character. The student in the hot seat shouldn't be given much time to plan responses, though the class may have built up quite a bit of background knowledge previously.

Problem-solving activities

These types of task usually require collaborative effort to complete. There is no correct answer but students are often called upon to explain or justify their decisions. Some common examples are described below.

Rank ordering. Students must reach a consensus about the relative importance of particular ideas, values or items. For example, in a unit on natural disasters, they might be asked to imagine they were being evacuated from their homes because of a cyclone. Working on their own initially, they make a prioritised list of five items they would take with them. They then meet in a group to reach agreement over one list of five items.

Design tasks. Collaborative design tasks encourage students to talk constructively, as long as the criteria of the task are clearly established. Many teachers construct a design brief to make their expectations clear, including such details as the product, the purpose, the materials and techniques, and the time available. The brief can also be used for evaluating finished products (see Fig. 2.5 for an example).

Design and construct a model for the improved playground in area 5.

The playground is to be used by young children attending playgroup as well as K–6 students, and for occasional school and community events.

The completed design should include existing facilities as well as more shade and a greater range of activities.

The model should be approximately one metre square and should be made from a variety of scrap and reused materials.

FIG. 2.5. EXAMPLE OF A DESIGN BRIEF

Worksheets. A carefully designed worksheet gives groups of students a measure of autonomy during problem-solving tasks, as well as fostering their language development. It will outline some problem or information gap to be solved and will usually allow for open-ended answers. It should be based on a common experience like an excursion or a shared text — for example, the playground observation worksheet reproduced as Fig. 2.6. Here students had identified the typical elements of children's playgrounds (e.g. swings, trees and litter bins) and grouped them according to function (shade, activities, aesthetics) in a joint construction with their teacher. They then used the worksheet to evaluate a number of playgrounds. Transcripts of the talk which featured prominently in the activity show a rich use of language centred on design and the built environment, and a high degree of interaction among the students without the need or distraction of the teacher's continual presence.

Playground Location: **Chapel St**

Criteria	How ?	very poor 1	not good 2	OK 3	good 4	excelent 5
Type and Variety of Activities	swings slide basketball nras				✓	
Safety	walls wooden fences grass ruber mats sand			✓		
Shade	trees walls huts		✗		✓	
Amenities (toilets, food, water)	bubbers garbage bin barbecu picnctabbls		✓		✓	
Attractiveness	Safty equipmnt, Seat, shade					✓
Access for disabled people	Yes safty path briges					✓
Space	Yes cont Picnic area path				✓✓	

FIG. 2.6. A WORKSHEET FOR ASSESSING PLAYGROUNDS

Some points to consider when designing tasks for talk

When they're using a particular type of communicative task for the first time, teachers often find that it doesn't work as well as they'd hoped. However, activities which don't succeed at first can be modified for subsequent use. Many teachers find checklists useful for designing successful oral language activities — here's an example:

> *Is talking necessary?*
>
> *Have students been provided with models of the language requirements of the task?*
>
> *Does the activity build on previous knowledge?*
>
> *Does the activity stimulate students' interest and engagement?*
>
> *Do students have to think and process information to contribute to the task?*
>
> *Do students know where to get assistance if they need it?*
>
> *Has enough time been allocated for students to complete the activity?*
>
> *Are all students involved?*
>
> (from Bremner 1995)

Of course, teachers do not consciously design all the spoken language activities that occur in their classrooms. Nevertheless making time to design and implement communicative tasks on a regular basis will help to provide a range of learning experiences, as well as opportunities for observation and assessment.

A sample unit of work

Fig. 2.7 reconstructs a unit of work on Leisure which was undertaken with two Year 3 classes in an urban area. Many of the children spoke languages other than English at home, and the school was classified as disadvantaged. The unit was collaboratively planned and taught by the classroom teachers and the ESL teacher over several weeks. At the same time the children were engaged in language and literacy activities clustered around the theme of leisure.

Although the unit was a part of a wider curriculum, the teachers wanted to work within the context of Science and Technology to develop understandings about the built environment and the process of design. They were also keen to explore with their students some of the ways in which decisions are made about the built environment and how informed community action can help shape local planning.

Worksheets and the design brief (Fig. 2.5) were used to scaffold activities. The teachers were very conscious of their students' language needs. The unit design provided for many oral language activities, although the emphasis throughout was on talk as process as students build up shared

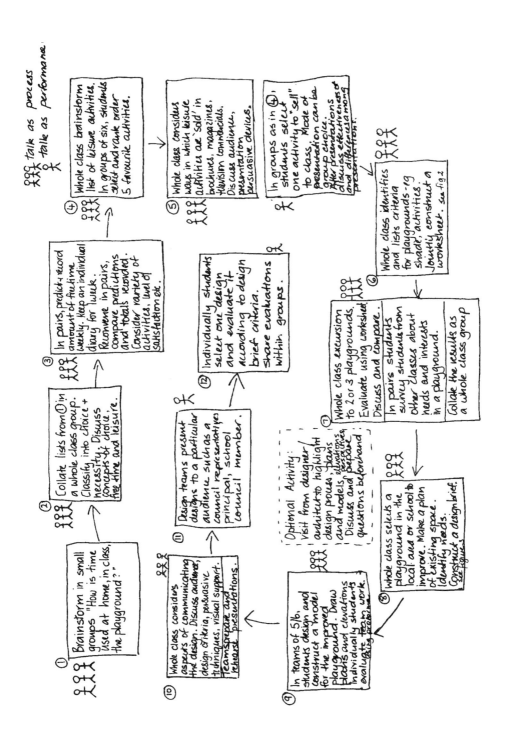

talk as process
talk as performance

① Brainstorm in small groups "How is time used at home, in class, the playground?"

② Collate lists from ① in a whole class group. Classify into choice + necessity. Discuss concepts of choice, free time and leisure.

③ In pairs, predict record amount of free time weekly. Keep an individual diary for week. Reconvene in pairs, compare predictions and totals recorded. Consider variety of activities, level of satisfaction etc.

④ Whole class brainstorm list of leisure activities. In groups of six, students select and rank order 5 favourite activities.

⑤ Whole class considers ways in which leisure activities are 'sold' in brochures, magazines, television commercials. Discuss audience, presentation, persuasive devices.

⑥ In groups as in ④, students select one activity to "sell" to class. Mode of presentation can be group choice. After presentations discuss effectiveness of and differences among presentations.

⑥ Whole class identifies and lists criteria for playgrounds - eg shade, activities. Jointly construct a worksheet. see fig.2

⑦ Whole class excursion to 2 or 3 playgrounds. Evaluate using worksheet. Discuss and compare. In pairs students survey students from other classes about needs and interests in a playground. Collate the results as a whole class group.

⑧ Whole class selects a playground in the local area or school to improve. Make a plan of existing space. Identify needs. Construct a design brief. see figure 3

⑨ In teams of 5/6, students design and construct a model for the improved playground. Draw plans and elevations individually. students evaluate team work.

⑩ Whole class considers aspects of communicating the design. Discuss audience, design criteria, persuasive techniques, visual support. Teams prepare and rehearse presentations.

⑪ Design teams present designs to a particular audience such as a council representative, principal, school council member.

⑫ Individually students select one design and evaluate it according to design brief criteria. Share evaluations within groups.

Optional Activity: Visit from designer/architect to highlight design process, plans and models, elevations, perspectives. Discuss and prepare questions beforehand.

FIG. 2.7. OUTLINE PLAN OF A UNIT ON LEISURE

knowledge and the technical language of the topic. Activities such as the initial brainstorming of activities, the rank ordering task, the playground excursion and the construction of models were rich in opportunities for students to talk to each other. There were also moments when teaching points about language and participation could be made and were made. The tasks in which talk was more careful or formal, such as selling the leisure activities and presenting designs, required quite explicit modelling.

The original unit design was subject to negotiation based on the students' interest and the teachers' judgement during implementation. The reconstruction presented here includes all resulting changes, as well as others made on more mature reflection, yet it does not differ significantly from the original. The balance of process and performance talk was one which the teachers were satisfied met the needs of these young students for this particular topic. In addition, using a range of formal and informal strategies, they were able not only to assess the students' talk in a variety of situations but also to use this talk as a means of assessing the students' understanding of the topic. Listening to students evaluating playgrounds and planning and presenting designs enabled them to judge the degree of control each student had over the conceptual and linguistic understandings involved. In the next chapter we'll look more closely at some means of assessing oral language.

Acknowledgement

I am grateful to Stephanie Searle and Tracey Thollar at Belmore South Public School for the use of material from their Leisure unit, which was developed with the support and resources of the Metropolitan East Disadvantaged Schools Program.

3

Assessing oral language

TINA SHARPE

We use oral language for different purposes, which naturally lead to different types of speaking and listening. One type is the *interactional*, used to develop and maintain social relationships — it's the language of the home, social gatherings and the playground. Another is the *transactional*, used for the transfer of information. Gaining control over this type is critical for students because it's the language of learning and predominates in the classroom.

Obviously listening and speaking are interdependent — both are required for any successful exchange, interactional or transactional — but there are differences between the two which need to be taken into account in the planning of assessment tasks. Some of these differences are noted below.

Components of listening

The ability to listen is something we all take for granted; we rarely think about the complex processes our brain goes through in order to make sense of what we hear. One result is that the assessment of listening skills is usually incidental to an activity. We only focus on them when there's some breakdown in meaning; otherwise we assume that they're developing. The successful completion of a task (e.g. following an instruction) is the usual way we recognise that a student has understood a message. But is this enough? How can we be sure that a student isn't merely 'parroting' answers without any real comprehension of what's happening or being learned? To make sure, we need to design more formal assessment tasks (e.g. completing a matrix), and to do this effectively we need to know something of what actually happens during the listening process.

For comprehension to take place, the listener needs to select what he or she will listen to, extract meaning from it and then respond to it in some way or other. To do this they need, according to Widdowson (1983):

- background knowledge — factual, sociocultural and procedural
- knowledge of the context of situation
- knowledge of the language system — semantic, syntactic and phonological.

For example, if we ask students to fill in a diary or timetable on the basis of our saying '9 a.m. Tuesday is PE time', we're assuming that they know what PE means, what a timetable sheet is used for and to how fill one in (factual, sociocultural and procedural knowledge), as well as how to separate sounds into words that make sense (language knowledge).

Listeners must also be able to vary their listening according to the situation. For example, if we're listening to a weather report because we're flying to Darwin the next day, we'll focus on the weather details for that region and not be much concerned about the details for Melbourne or Perth. Likewise, when listening to an explanation of a procedure we're quite familiar with, such as using a video recorder, we'll listen less intently or 'half' listen as a reinforcement, only intensifying our focus if some fresh piece of information crops up.

However, this ability to vary our listening is a skill we can't simply assume that students have picked up. Asking them to perform a variety of tasks, such as listening to a short talk and then summarising the key points, or relaying messages to another person (e.g. 'whispers'), is a useful way of assessing their ability in this area.

Components of speaking

The different functions of spoken language are distinguished by the use of different kinds of language. Interactional usage is characterised by lots of fillers like *um* and *er* and non-specific references like *this* and *it*. Speech usually occurs in short bursts and is often repetitive. It's also unpredictable as it can easily go off on tangents with expressions like *that reminds me . . .* or *by the way . . .* In contrast, transactional language tends to employ longer, more coherent structures, to avoid repetition, and to use vocabulary specific to the topic. Teacher talk is predominantly transactional, and unless we're assessing a student's ability to interact socially with peers, it's the trans-actional element in our students' language use which we assess.

When we think about students' spoken language, we need to consider not just what is said (the *meaning*) but how it is said (the *mechanics*). *Meaning* relates to such concerns as the relevance of the information communicated and the logical progression of ideas. As teachers, we've long been aware of the importance of background knowledge in comprehending printed texts, but we've often overlooked its importance in the successful negotiation of a spoken exchange. Brown and Yule (1983, pp. 60–61) have pointed out that spoken language occurs in a context of situation. Anyone speaking or listening 'encounters that context with a set of stereotypical knowledge which he has been building up from the time he first acquired language as an infant in the culture. He is predisposed to construct expectations on the basis of this stereotypical knowledge.' They postulate that the context of situation contains the following components:

- speaker & listener
- place & time
- genre & topic
- co-text (i.e. the other parts of the text, both before and after the part currently in play).

In these terms, making meaning depends upon awareness and successful manipulation of the context of situation.

The *mechanics* are concerned basically with accuracy and fluency. *Accuracy* refers to the precision and freedom from error of the language being used. *Fluency* means that the language is flowing smoothly and easily; it's a term concerned with the duration of speech and with pronunciation. However, *pronunciation* is not just a matter of uttering individual sounds, for it also embraces a number of other elements like stress, pausing, speed, pitch, volume and intonation.

Stress refers to the energy with which a word is spoken. In English it's usually the stressed syllable in a word or a stressed word in a sentence which carries the primary message.

Pausing is commonly used before an important word to mark its importance.

Speed of delivery varies. We tend to slow down when we want to emphasise something and to speed up when we're elaborating a point or making an aside.

Pitch is usually used to express emotion. When we're excited, our pitch rises.

Volume refers to variations in loudness. It is not the same as stress, for it's quite possible to vary the stress without any perceptible difference in volume.

Intonation comprises the pattern of pitch changes in speech. A downward intonation indicates that a message is complete, while an upward intonation indicates a question.

The range of assessment opportunities

Not only do we need to be aware of the different elements that can be assessed in oral language — we also have to consider the range of classroom contexts that provide opportunities for assessment. Meiers (1983) has categorised the many activities which include oral language as follows:

1 individual student talk – formal (e.g. a debate)
2 individual student talk – informal (e.g. an unsolicited recount of a family trip)
3 small group activities (e.g. a problem-solving task)
4 whole class activities (e.g. a class discussion)
5 games (e.g. jazz chants)
6 simulations and role plays (e.g. Hot Seat)
7 reading aloud
8 activities focusing awareness of spoken language (e.g. oral storytelling)
9 special presentations (e.g. a vote of thanks to a guest speaker).

Each of these activities offers opportunities to assess different aspects of oral language.

It can be helpful to think about talk in terms of a bi-directional continuum from spontaneous language to rehearsed or sculptured language. Fig. 3.1 shows a range of oral activities placed along this continuum, and also relates them to the transactional, interactional and poetic forms of language.

Rehearsed ←— More structured ←—Spontaneous —→ More Polished —→ Sculptured				
Debates	Interviews	Conversation	Role playing	Storytelling
Oral reports	Directions	Brainstorming	Improvising	Reader's theatre
Presentations	Instructions	Exploratory talk	Monologue	Prepared dramatic presentations
Transactional ←——————— Interactional ——————→ Poetic				

(adapted from Ontario Ministry of Education 1987)

FIG 3.1. THE ORAL LANGUAGE CONTINUUM

Spoken language can be assessed at any point along the continuum — from the observation of spontaneous talk during a relatively simple task, or

These students are negotiating the sharing of materials to complete a project.
Listening to groups at work can provide valuable information about students'
social and cognitive development.

while students are answering or asking questions, through to a formal criterion-referenced assessment of rehearsed talk, such as an explanation or a retelling. The criteria we choose will vary according to the formality of the task and whether it involves one-way or two-way communication. Some suggestions for developing criteria are given below.

TWO-WAY COMMUNICATION
- mutual trust and respect
- willingness to acknowledge and express feelings
- exploratory or speculative thinking
- willingness to venture ideas, take risks
- supportiveness
- development and extension of others' contributions
- appropriate questioning (e.g. to obtain information, to probe)
- use of responses to questions (e.g. in interviews)
- initiative in raising new or related issues

- leadership
- tenacity in pursuing ideas
- clarity of explanation
- persuasiveness
- attentive listening
- awareness of listeners' needs
- response to another's difficulties
- tact in resolving disagreement

ONE-WAY COMMUNICATION
- fluency
- confidence and self-possession
- animation
- effort to arouse and maintain interest
- effective use of voice (tone, pitch, stress, speed, pausing, intonation)
- clear expression of ideas
- logical presentation
- coherent argument
- persuasiveness
- willingness to express feelings and opinions where appropriate
- appropriateness of material and style for audience
- flexibility of style
- courteous and attentive listening
- critical listening

                              (adapted from Education Department of SA 1990, pp. 56–57)

When assessing oral language we should always bear in mind that students' performance and behaviour may be affected by the status of others who are part of the activity or observing it, and by their relationships with them. We should also avoid trying to assess a student's oral development on the basis of a single activity; assessment should be spread over a period of time and cover a range of contexts and a number of different purposes.

Tapes and proformas

Audio or video tapes are extremely useful for enhancing the accuracy of observation. Since they remain available for more detailed analysis at a later date, they take the pressure off the teacher trying to watch for a number of behaviours and criteria simultaneously. It's a good idea to record students regularly so that they become familiar with the process as part of classroom routine and overcome any tendency to 'act up' to the recorder.

Proformas can also be a great help as they provide a reminder of the kinds of behaviours and language structures we want to observe. However, it's often difficult to complete a proforma in detail at the first attempt, and then we risk omitting important information. In such cases it's particularly helpful to record the activity so that we can replay the tape later and add any details we may have missed.

Case study 1: spontaneous discussion and description

The rest of this chapter is devoted to case studies — examples of different tasks devised to assess students using oral language for a range of different purposes. In the first one, which involved four Year 1 children, the teacher orchestrated an activity which enabled her first to observe their spontaneous oral language in a small group situation, and then a slightly more rehearsed form of oral language when they described the activity.

All four children had been born in Australia. Sara (7) spoke English only, but Nathan (7) spoke some Italian to his grandparents, while Mitchell (6) had a Maltese-speaking grandmother who lived with him and his parents. Jacinta (6) spoke to her parents in English and they responded in both English and Indonesian (they spoke to each other in Indonesian).

The children were each given a Santa stencil to colour and cut out and make into a mask. They had cotton wool, a hole punch, string and coloured pencils, and they could make the mask any colour they liked. After a brief exchange about why they did or didn't like being recorded, they began to discuss what they had to do. In the following transcript they are represented by their initials, while 'T' stands for their teacher.

J: What else should I colour?
S: I don't know.
J: Oh well.
S: What else is red on um Santa?
J: I don't know what else is red on Santa.
M: Well, we don't really see.
S: That's it. You can colour his nose, his mouth . . .
J: What colour should that be?
T: What are they called?
S: Eyebrows.
T: What colour do you think?
J: Grey.
S: White, white.

J: Do you leave it?

M: Yes, because um because he has . . . like every time I watch a Santa um Claus he always has the white eyebrows.

T: Do you think the eyebrows might match the hair colour on the beard?

M: Yep.

T: They might all match?

M: Yep, yeah.

With the children thus engaged in an activity that became the natural focus of their talk, the teacher was able to observe a number of things. For example, the children knew the names of parts of the face (e.g. *mouth*, *eyebrows*), and Jacinta and Sara were able to ask questions using the correct form. Mitchell was able to give a reason for not colouring in Santa's eyebrows, based on his own observations of the world.

In the next excerpt we see the teacher asking questions to check whether the children understood the procedure for putting cotton wool on the stencil to make Santa's beard.

J: Do we have to cut out the black line?

T: No. What do you think we're going to put on the black lines?

S: Glue.

T: Cotton wool?

S: Yeah, all down there.

J: We put the glue down there?

T: Yes, that's good. So the lines show you where to put the glue . . . You put the glue on, OK?

M: Be careful it doesn't dry.

T: Jacinta, have a look at what Mitchell's done. Do you think you could do the same? What's he done?

J: Put glue on the line.

T: Put glue on the lines on what? *(J points to beard)* That's right.

Questioning enabled the teacher to make sure that Jacinta had understood the procedure for making the mask. Again the children used appropriate vocabulary for the task, and Mitchell's warning to Jacinta about letting the glue dry showed that he'd already had experience of using glue.

A few minutes later, when the children had finished their masks, the teacher asked them to pretend they were explaining the procedure to someone who didn't know how to make a mask at all. This is what each one said:

J: You use cotton wool to stick on the mask and then cut out the Santa Claus; then you put strings on it so you can put the mask on us.

M: You gotta have this piece of cardboard, and then you cut it out and you stick the glue on it, and you gotta cut the eyes out to er . . . so you can see, and um you can, you have to Ho Ho Ho . . . you have to tie . . . you have to measure the string so you can um put it on you, and um that's all.

S: You have to put holes with um the hole pumper, and you put the string through it so you can put the mask on. You got to stick glue for the beard, the pom pom and the moustache and a bit of the hat and you've got to colour it in . . . like you colour the hat in and the mouth, and if you want to you can colour in the nose and the mouth.

N: Well, first you have to colour in the hat red and then you cut it out, and then you put some glue on some lines, and then you use um cotton wool, and then you colour the nose and the mouth whatever colour you want, and then you put two holes so you can put the string on and . . . and then you can wear your mask.

Jacinta was broadly able to sequence the procedure, but she left out the first step (colouring in the stencil) and didn't provide any detail like cutting out the eyes. Her limited retelling, combined with her tentativeness and constant questioning to check on what she should do, indicated that she needed to be monitored fairly closely to ensure that she understood set tasks.

Mitchell sequenced the procedure correctly, adding a little humour, but like Jacinta's, his account was incomplete. Both children needed to hear more models of retelling an activity, and both would have benefited from scaffolding in the form of questions (e.g. *What's the first thing you did with the stencil? Where on the mask did you put the glue?*) to supply specific vocabulary and appropriate sequence words.

Sara sequenced the whole procedure backwards from last action to first. While this was quite logical in its way, it was something to watch for in the future.

Nathan does not appear in the transcripts of spontaneous talk because he preferred to work independently throughout. He worked slowly and methodically, and was the last to finish. His recount was the most detailed and was sequenced appropriately with words like *then* and *when*.

Case study 2: a spontaneous retelling

Fabrice (12) had been born in Mauritius and had come to Australia at the age of 5. He spoke French at home but could not read or write in French. He was read Robert Munsch's picture book *The Paper Bag Princess* and was then asked to retell the story without the book. His version is given below, and the teacher's assessment sheet is reproduced as Fig 3.2:

One day there was a girl that wanted to marry a Prince. And a dragon came and blew down the whole castle and took the Prince away. The dragon even blew her clothes. The princess had nothing else to wear but a old bag.

Fabrice

CRITERIA	COMMENTS	RATING 5 = very competent 0 = not yet competent
Success in task: e.g. • comprehensibility of content • sequenced correctly • logical progression • relevance of ideas	able to retell with all key incidents included – sequenced correctly	(5) 4 3 2 1 0
Appropriate vocabulary: e.g. • descriptive words • variety	problems with *forresters, aten, lied* – minimal use of descriptive words from the book (e.g. didn't use *fiery, slammed, smashed, fantastic*)	5 4 (3) 2 1 0
Accuracy of language structures: e.g. • word order • word endings • correct pronouns	incorrect article used – *a old bag*	(5) 4 3 2 1 0
Length and coherence of text: e.g. • appropriate length for task • ideas related to topic • logical relationship of ideas developed within text	no evident problems	(5) 4 3 2 1 0
Fluency and pronunciation: e.g. • smooth flow of words • correct intonation • minimal hesitations and fillers (*um, er*) • pauses	fluent retelling, few hesitations, appeared confident – tendency to mumble towards end of sentence – stress on important words	5 (4) 3 2 1 0
Interaction with listener and listener response: e.g. • maintaining eye contact • engaging listener	looked away at times	5 (4) 3 2 1 0

OVERALL COMMENTS: Competent retelling of story shows understanding of sequence and significance of events. However, limited use of descriptive vocabulary and irregular verb forms shows need to develop language in this area.

FIG 3.2. ASSESSMENT OF A SPONTANEOUS ORAL RETELLING

The Princess went after the dragon — there was nothing left but old bones. The Princess found a cave, knocked on the door and the dragon's nose popped out and the dragon said, 'I have aten the whole castle today but I don't . . . I really like Princesses but I don't want to eat. Come back tomorrow.' Next time and the Princess knocked again. The dragon popped out and said the same thing. Then the Princess said, 'Is it true that you can blow down ten forrester?' and the dragon said 'Yes' and he took a BIG breath and blew the forresters, the forresters down, fifty forresters. And then said and then took another deep breath and blew down a hundred forresters. The princess said, 'Is it true you can fly around the world in ten seconds?' and he jumped up and flew around the world in ten, ten, ten . . . seconds.

He was really tired when he came back and said and did it again but this time it took twenty seconds. He lied on the ground and was so tired he couldn't get up. The Princess said 'Hey dragon' and the dragon just laid there. She put her face right in his ears and screamed out 'Hey dragon!'. The dragon didn't move. She went into the cave and saw the Prince but the Prince said, 'You have ashes all over you,' and the Princess called him a toad and they didn't get married.

The same task was given to Lucas (12), a native speaker of English, to compare his language development with Fabrice's. Lucas completed the task successfully, as Fabrice had, but he was able to call on a more extensive vocabulary, some of which was not in the story (e.g. *smashed the castle, she followed the trail of all burnt grass and horses' bones, she kept persisting*).

Case study 3: a spontaneous technical description and explanation

Learning technical language and gaining control of it is critical for all students, as those who fail to understand and use it soon become disadvantaged in every curriculum area. Thus, as well as assessing students' development from spontaneous to rehearsed oral language, we need to check on their ability to transfer information from one field to another. Can they apply new learning to a new situation? In this case study we watch one student successfully doing so.

The student concerned, Edward (9), spoke English mainly, but sometimes spoke Indonesian to his parents. In common with the rest of his class he had been working on a unit on Tools. For this taped assessment task he was given a familiar object (a pair of scissors) and asked to describe it and explain how it worked. This was the result:

E: Well this is a tool and um . . .

T: Can you tell me what it is?

E: It's scissors and it's things that you um . . . can cut um . . . like you can use this
     for cutting things like cardboard . . . and . . . um . . . This is called a tool because
     um you use hands um   It's not a machine because it doesn't work just like

uh . . . it doesn't go by itself like doing it or anything like that.

T: Can you describe it for me?

E: Well, well it's got a pointy end that's really sharp, it's got a um oh got a hand . . . or something.

T: A handle, yeah?

E: Yeah um . . .

T: What does the handle look like?

E: A handle is like um like you hold on it, and you use two um of these holes so you can put your hand through it.

T: And what about the action of the scissors?

E: You just like cut like that and there's noises *(does action)*.

T: What does 'like that' mean?

E: Oh, oh it makes noises and . . .

T: How do you move your hand?

E: Well you just go up and down.

T: Right, and that makes it move.

E: Yeah.

T: How does it hold together?

E: Well you just put it in the hole and just go like that *(demonstrates)*.

T: What stops the two bits falling apart?

E: Um . . .

T: The two blades, what stops them coming apart?

E: Um, um the nail.

T: The nail or the screw?

E: Yeah, the screw.

The transcript shows that Edward had understood the concept of a tool and was able to use some technical terminology (e.g. *tool* and *machine*). He explained why the pair of scissors was not a machine by referring to a characteristic of machines (i.e. *it doesn't go by itself*). However, the transcript also shows that he needed to develop more technical language as he was dependent upon actions to help describe the scissors.

Next Edward was asked to describe and explain how a small hand-held mouli grater worked. The purpose of repeating the activity like this was to assess the transference of new information he had been working on (both concepts and technical vocabulary) to an unfamiliar object. During this activity he was sitting with another student, Carmen.

Edward was handed the grater broken down into its components, and this is how he reacted:

E: Well this looks like a hard one and maybe it's . . . probably put something . . . that's really oval um . . . and then you probably like turn it around and it goes like little pieces and comes out.

T: Can you describe for me all the different parts?

E: Um . . .

T: I mean what does it look like?

E: This part, it's a handle and it's used for rolling food and um um um um . . .

T: Do you want to give it back to me and I'll put the pieces back together again and you might have a better go? *(Mouli grater is assembled)* Now would you like to describe what it looks like?

E: Oh yeah, it's like a lawn mower. It got like a handle thing and the thing that um and that's all.

T: What's that thing that you roll around?

E: It's a handle and um this is for food and probably for putting little pieces like that and you put it in here.

T: Have you heard the word 'grate' or 'grater'? *(E hesitates)* Do you know what to grate food means?

E: No.

T: Do you know, Carmen?

C: To like . . . say you've got cheese or something, you can . . . you can rub it up and down on a grater and it makes small pieces.

E: Oh yeah.

T: Now do you want to feel the inside of that? Now feel the outside. What do you think the function of that cylinder might be?

E: Oh yeah, um the inside is a bit smooth but this one is a bit more bumpier than the inside.

T: So what might it do to food?

E: Cut it into little pieces.

T: What's the word for cutting it into little pieces?

E: Um grate.

T: That's it, good boy!

Edward once again demonstrated a limited technical vocabulary which affected his ability to describe the object accurately. Direct questioning by his teacher helped to scaffold him, but this transcript reinforces the case for more work on developing language for description.

Some of the characteristics Edward displayed were typical of an ESL learner. Although he had a basic understanding of the concepts being taught (i.e. tools), his limited language resources affected his performance in the task. His limitations also point to the importance of teachers recognising the demands placed on students to use transactional language in the classroom — so different from the interactional language they use at home or in the playground. However, recognising these demands (as well as students' particular needs) has little point unless the recognition has a direct impact on what subsequently happens in the classroom. A close linkage between assessment and programming is essential.

Case study 4: justifying an opinion – moving from spontaneous to rehearsed language

The final case study highlights the development of students' oral language between Years 1 and 6. We can see some development as students progress from Year 1 (the mask-making transcript) to Year 4 (the description and explanation of tools). The transcript below shows a further development, with students required to state and justify opinions about an issue. Apart from an obvious difference in the length of their utterances, the four Year 6 students exhibit more precision in their language through the use of noun groups (e.g. *the village people*, *polluted water*, *the tailings*) and causal connectives (e.g. *therefore* and *because*). The students involved were:

Jessica (11), born in Australia. Her parents spoke Maltese to her; she sometimes responded in Maltese but more often in English.

Rodrigo (11), born in Nicaragua. He came to Australia at the age of 2 and spoke mostly Spanish.

Anthony (12) spoke English only. His parents came from Egypt and spoke Italian, which he could understand.

Leonie (12) spoke English only.

The whole class had been studying issues arising from BHP's mining at Ok Tedi in Papua New Guinea. They had seen a documentary video and read newspaper reports. Working in small groups, they were discussing whether there should be mining at Ok Tedi. Each group's task was to present their opinion to the rest of the class. After the groups had had a few minutes discussion, the teacher handed out copies of a fact sheet to assist in their presentations. The fact sheet listed key points developed by class and teacher over a period of time.

This is how the discussion of our focus group proceeded:

J: I remember when all the water, like all the water in the river, was full of sand and it made the water all muddy . . . the water level rise because of the sand.

A: And there's this lady and she says the plants are all dying because of the lack of oxygen in the soil, because there's so much waste from the copper mine, and there's um . . . the mountains got shorter because they've mined it all away.

J: And they're worried because the water is rising – they don't want their village to drown.

L: And they've got polluted water – they don't have much fresh water – the tailings . . .

J: And they need the water to drink and all that.

A: Yeah, they're drinking out of the well but . . .

L: Yeah.

A: I reckon it's a bit slack for all the people because the government is just doing it because they want money and the villages are suffering, but the government doesn't really care.

L: The government probably does care but like he's just doing it so Papua New Guinea — for money, so like they're in our standards a bit.

J: Then like when they've got enough money, they can clean like still the waters and do whatever they want to do.

A: Yeah, it's a problem to clean 'cause the stuff is all the way through.

L: On the show it says that it's only a short-term problem so . . .

J: I think I go against it, it's easier to go against it.

A: And it's not right.

R: For the village people. *(Students are given a fact sheet by the teacher)*

L: Do you want to go for or against it?

J: Against it, against it.

L: We'll have a vote. Who wants against it?

A: I think everyone'll go against it.

L: BHP in Papua New Guinea . . . *(she begins to write)*

R: That's the first person.

A: First we need a list of all the things we're going to say.

J: Just say 'We don't think . . . '

L: Just say that sure Papua New Guinea need money but people can get it in other ways.

A: If they didn't pollute the water supply they could just get the timber or maybe grow fruit.

J: Yeah, we're going against that — you list that *(points to a fact on the sheet)*.

A: They could grow cotton or something.

L: Like it's unfair for the people living in the village because they have to live without clean water and they can't wash their clothes properly, or they can wash their clothes but in dirty water, showering and cleaning . . . and then because they don't have an education.

A: They just — the government probably told them 'Oh you'll make money,' but they didn't know what they were doing.

J: OK, so they've no education — therefore when they visit another country or when they come to live in Australia and they want to get a job, it'll be very hard to get one because they don't have the education to.

L: Instead of saying that, you could say that because they've no education they weren't able to read the contracts and so um . . . like anyone could've just said anything.

A: Like they said 'Oh you'll get lots of money out of this,' and if they told them what was actually going to happen about pollution I don't think they would've signed, or some of them would've signed but not . . .

R: Yeah.

A: The majority of people said that they shouldn't be doing it.

L: OK, so what've we got? The Papua New Guinea people have no education, there-
     fore they weren't able to read the contracts and could've been told anything . . .

The discussion continued for a few more minutes until the group had drafted their final statement:

Sure PNG need money but they can make it doing other things for example grow a timber farm, grow crops. The PNG people have no education therefore they were not able to read the contract and could have been told anything. The Government cares about the people but he is destroying the flora and fauna. Although he is making money it will take more money to fix up the environment in PNG. When BHP are mining the tailings they are flowing down the mountain and into the river not into the tailings dam. When the trees are being cut down they have less oxygen. BHP cut 400m of the mountains down which flows into the river and the water level has risen. For all of the reasons above we think this a very unfair situation and the government should stop mining.

The transcript shows that Jessica, Leonie and Anthony engaged quickly and enthusiastically with the task. They began by referring to the documentary they'd seen and there was some discussion about whether the problem was short- or long-term. Anthony had strong views about the issue (*it's not right*), while Jessica began by seeing the problem as one that could be fixed (*when they've got enough money, they can clean like still the waters and do whatever they want to*). Nevertheless she decided to go against the mining — *it's easier to go against it.*

The fourth member of the group, Rodrigo, made little contribution to the discussion, and the teacher observed that often he didn't even seem to be listening. The difficulty he appeared to experience with the task showed that he needed careful monitoring to ensure progress in his cognitive and language development.

Although the group had had previous experience in preparing an opinion text, in this case their introductory sentence was too spoken-like. However, their final sentence was appropriate. They clearly needed some guidance on punctuation, and their text needed more work to give it cohesion, for the facts, though relevant, were not linked in a logical cause-and-effect sequence. Other groups' oral presentations, reproduced below, show a greater awareness of the need for more formal language and a logical connection of ideas. This is particularly evident in Group 3's text.

Group 1

The people in our group are against BHP mining in PNG. Reasons for this are that the waste is polluting the main river. Animals are dying — all because BHP want to make money.

The government says that they need the money but the people who actually live by the river have no say. Floods are ruining the forest because the river water is rising because there is so much waste in the river.

Those are most of the reasons why we believe that BHP mining in the Ok Tedi river is wrong.

Group 2

We oppose the mining of the Ok Tedi river because we think BHP are taking advantage of the village people. The village people don't know how to read or write and BHP forced them to sign the contract without the natives knowing what they were signing. The village people have no say in what the government is doing to their land. BHP are dirtying the rivers and the river level is rising.

Group 3

Our group strongly agree with BHP mining in the Ok Tedi river. Because BHP have put a lot of money into the country. It has built schools, hospitals and it has raised their life expectancy by 30 years. This is also giving the PNG country a lot more money to run the country. This is helping the country and it is giving them a chance that they might not have. It is giving the country a positive lifestyle.

Conclusion

In this chapter we've looked at some of the different purposes for which we use oral language. These purposes place different demands on both listener and speaker, and so when we're assessing students' oral abilities, we need to know exactly what we're looking for. In developing assessment criteria we should consider if the communication is one-way or two-way, spontaneous or rehearsed, interactional, transactional or poetic. We also need to realise the importance of giving students a wide range of opportunities to develop their oral language skills. These can subsequently be assessed, formally and informally, and the information gained can make a vital contribution to our planning and teaching, leading to relevant and effective learning for all our students.

Acknowledgement

I would like to acknowledge the invaluable assistance given by Karen Watterson, ESL teacher at St Agnes' Primary School, Matraville, in organising classes and teaching the activities from which the transcripts are drawn. My thanks also to the staff at St. Agnes' for cooperating so willingly during the collection of materials.

4

Making the most of traditional newstime

VICTORIA ROBERTS

VIVIENNE NICOLL

For many teachers, particularly in the early years of school, newstime is an important component of the class oral language program. It gives children opportunities to share personal experiences with their peers (hence linking home and school), and it's a relatively non-threatening way of introducing young children to the experience of addressing an audience. But unless it's carefully planned and regularly evaluated, it can easily become a waste of the class's time, and may even have some quite unintended negative results. So in this chapter we have outlined a few ways to ensure that traditional newstime is a valuable part of the day.

Providing a structure

Like any other classroom practice, newstime needs to be planned and programmed. If teachers want children to be informative and interesting speakers and attentive listeners, they have to provide scaffolding — they have to structure newstime for success.

Newstime should change over the year, developing as the children develop, and should be integrated as far as possible with other aspects of the class program. It needn't always be personal — whilst there's a secure place for oral recounts of children's experiences, it's also desirable to widen the concept of newstime to embrace activities in other key learning areas, school and local happenings, children's opinions on current issues, and the excitement of special national or international events. For example, when children are exposed to constant media coverage (and possibly family discussions) during the Olympic Games or a federal election, newstime can easily be focused on these recurrent contests. At other times it can help a class come to terms with traumatic public events. Many children will encounter such things accidentally through snippets of adult conversation or glimpses of television news footage. A sensitively managed discussion during newstime can help to reassure them and place painful events in a broader perspective.

As well as planning the 'content' of newstime, teachers need to have some kind of plan for teaching appropriate speaking and listening skills. The classroom is generally the first forum in which children are expected to speak 'in public', and most find it a rather different experience from the conversational exchanges they are used to with family or friends.

It's also worth noting that newstime provides excellent opportunities for the informal assessment of talking and listening to amplify judgements of children's language use made on the basis of more formal tasks (see previous chapter).

Learning to be an interesting speaker

Although we tend to take it for granted that the impromptu telling of 'news' comes easily to children, not all of them are good news-givers by nature. So what happens to those who aren't naturally eloquent — are they destined always to have speaking labelled 'satisfactory' in their written reports? Well, no; and the remedy is to teach speaking skills in the same way as you teach others. Below are some ideas for doing this that you might begin with.

Being prepared

It's the lucky few who can extemporise to an audience without any preparation — most of us can't. At school, however, if children are given some notice that their turn for news is coming up, or that news will be devoted to a particular topic, they can think over what to say and 'rehearse' it in their heads or under their breath. They can also be encouraged to prepare and rehearse their news at home, particularly as many parents enjoy this way of supporting their children. Nevertheless you should make it clear to parents that such preparation doesn't mean scripted news which children learn by heart, or anything like drilling in front of a mirror!

Some teachers find it helps to show 'how to give news' by modelling examples and providing prompts to scaffold what's being talked about. Prompts for recounting a personal experience, for example, might take this form:

When?   Who?   Where?   What?   (How?)   (Why?)

Prompts for contributing to a discussion might be:

State what you think.   *I think that . . .*
Give some reasons.   *. . . because . . . Secondly . . .*

If the prompts are displayed on charts, children can use them at any time to plan or rehearse what they are going to say (i.e. for a recount of a personal experience, when it happened, who was involved, where it happened and what happened).

Speaking clearly and looking at the audience

It may seem obvious to adults that you should maintain eye contact with an audience, speak loudly enough to be heard and choose a pace that's comfortable for your listeners, neither racing nor limping. However, none of these points is necessarily self-evident to children, and it's worth spending some time making sure that they've grasped their importance. A summary chart placed in sight of where news is to be given makes a useful reminder (see Fig. 4.1 for an example).

GOOD SPEAKERS	GOOD LISTENERS
speak clearly	sit still
look at their audience	look at the speaker
show interest in their topic	do not interrupt

FIG. 4.1. A PAIR OF SAMPLE CHARTS

Learning to be an attentive listener

Almost every child wants to be a speaker; not so many find it easy to listen. Yet every speaker benefits from an attentive audience. So, as well as providing a framework for news-givers, you may well need to teach the whole class some audience skills. For example, you might demonstrate that while news is being given, good listeners:

- look at the speaker
- don't interrupt
- sit still.

You might also demonstrate ways that good listeners can show their interest afterwards — either by making a comment:

- to show appreciation – *I liked your news*
- to show empathy – *That's happened to me too and I know how you felt*

- to acknowledge the experience – *I've seen that movie*

or by asking a question:

- to seek further information – *How long did it take to get there?*
- to seek clarification – *Did you mean . . . ?*
- to elicit the news-giver's feelings – *Did you enjoy your visit?*

Once these audience skills have been made explicit, they should be displayed on charts and practised by the children, perhaps working first in pairs. The prompts charts for news-giving which include the WH-question beginnings can also act as prompts for the kinds of questions that might be asked, particularly after recounts of personal experiences. Attentive and active listening should praised, particularly early in the year.

Running a news session

Research by Robyn Cusworth (1995) confirms that some teachers don't see newstime as an occasion for focused teaching. However, if newstime is to be treated as a significant component of the oral language program, it can't also be treated as an opportunity for the teacher to get some housekeeping done while the children run the session themselves. The teacher always has to be a participant (at the very least, a model of attentive listening) and sometimes a model of how news might be given. If housekeeping has to be done first thing in the morning, then newstime should be postponed till later in the day.

Newstime sessions shouldn't be overlong. Good listening, however 'active', remains in important respects so passive that children can't be expected to sustain it for extended periods. In planning the length of sessions, teachers will of course consider the age, experience and skills of the children involved, but they should also think about the news 'content'. A series of 'On the weekend . . . ' recounts may soon become repetitive and boring, whereas, given some preparatory thought and a variety of opinions, a 'discussion' about what foods should be sold at the canteen may hold children's attention for longer than expected.

Prior to a session, the teacher may revise the prompts appropriate to the kind of speaking planned for the day, or draw attention to charts that remind children of news etiquette. When the session's over, she may ask the children to say how they think it went and why. For instance, it might well be that outside noises or an interruption for a message broke listeners' concentration, or that a speaker wasn't well enough prepared. Reflecting on such things draws children's attention to the factors which make for a good oral presentation.

Varying newstime formulas

Many teachers provide 'rituals' to structure the newstime session. For example, the news-giver may begin by saying 'Good morning, class', to which the class replies 'Good morning, Sam'. There are many ways of varying a procedure like this, such as introducing and discussing a series of alternative greetings over the year.

Greetings and other highly predictable elements like requests for questions can also give children an opportunity to practise languages other than English — both those taught at the school and those used by class members. For example, there's a Year 1 class in which the news-giver usually begins in Indonesian: *Selamat pagi, anak anak* (Good morning, children). The class responds *Selamat pagi, Katy.* The news is then given in English, but expressions and comments like these are used regularly:

Ada paertanyaan?	Are there any questions?
Ya, Joel	Yes, Joel
Bagus, baik	Great, good
Baik sekali	Very good
Hebat	Terrific
Maaf	Sorry

The importance young children place on news

Young children don't see newstime as 'oral language development'. In the early years of school they see it as their 'three minutes of fame' each week, and this has many implications for their teachers.

When news is poorly received

A poorly received news item can be devastating to a child's self-esteem. If the expectation is that the audience will respond with questions or comments and yet no-one does, the news-giver will probably feel a failure and be reluctant to perform next time around. Alert teachers will head off the danger by initiating questions and comments or otherwise encouraging the class to respond.

When a turn is missed

Many teachers allocate children particular days for their newstime, so that five or six have news on Monday, another five or six on Tuesday, and so on. Certainly this system helps planning and allows children to be prepared, and it also contains the news session. However, it does have a major problem — the dreaded 'missed turn'. When the class goes on an excursion or has an assembly for a special occasion, or when there's a public holiday, children who've planned a particular item and built up great expectations for it can feel enormously let down and unhappy — even when the teacher has warned them that they will miss their turn. Should this happen often enough, children will soon come to see that preparation doesn't count and newstime is just a time-filler. They may also feel cheated and begin to learn that the education system has its own injustices.

Teachers should at least have a contingency plan to cater for this problem. However, a better solution is to replace allocated news *days* with allocated news *groups* (e.g. the blue group, the yellow group, etc.). A simple chart with a moveable arrow indicates whose turn is coming up next. The advantages of this system are that you can have more than five groups and therefore shorter sessions, and that children don't expect to have a turn every week or on a specific day. If you want children to prepare for news, you simply remind a group that it's their turn for news tomorrow and tell them that preparation for it can be their homework.

The greater flexibility of the system also allows you to slot in 'special news' when something out of the ordinary occurs — the baby tooth that's at last come out, the new sister, the broken arm and the trip to casualty. And, as children get older, there can be a place on the class noticeboard for them to record a request for newstime space that afternoon or the next day, maybe to show the lizard they've found or to tell about how they went in the combined schools' athletics carnival.

One-upmanship

Some teachers call newstime 'show and tell', perhaps on the assumption that young children are more relaxed talking about the here and now. But even when it isn't called show and tell, the class culture can soon turn newstime into a 'bring and brag' occasion, especially if children discover that they gain more kudos or interest from bringing an enviable possession. This pressure to bring something new or 'big' each time too often means getting caught up in an anxious spiral of material competition, till eventually some children don't want to give news at all. Even recounts of weekend outings can become an opportunity for one-upmanship. On the other hand, children risk ridicule if they bring in a prized possession that's not seen as 'cool', or something they've drawn or made at home.

Teachers can easily avoid such damaging competitiveness by re-examining the *purposes* of newstime and setting broad topics. For example, there could be a week's focus on:

- your favourite food
- ways you spend your spare time at home
- a book you've enjoyed reading this month

- bringing something made of wood, showing its purpose and explaining how you think it was made.

The language used in show-and-tell sessions is necessarily context-bound, relying heavily on the presence of objects. However, topics like those listed above are calculated to move children towards a more reflective and distanced use of language.

The content of newstime can also be drawn from current class work in any key learning area. Children can 'show and tell' things they've designed and made, experiments they've undertaken, or information they've discovered (and how they went about discovering it). And, in Chapter 7, Kathleen Rushton explains how she uses a set of games during newstime to help her teach Aboriginal students the basic structures of various text types, including recount, description, procedure and narrative. What's most important is that newstime has purposes shared between teacher and children, and that the children are familiar with what they're talking about (i.e. the content or 'field knowledge' of the news).

Alternatives to whole class news

So far this chapter has focused on the traditional newstime session, with the speaker addressing the whole class seated on the floor. Provided they're properly scaffolded, such sessions can have value in preparing children for more formal oral presentations (e.g. giving a prepared two-minute talk, debating, assembly items, or introducing a guest speaker), and for being an appreciative audience in different situations (e.g. readers theatre, assemblies, or visits from artists and writers).

There are, however, a number of alternatives to a whole class setting for newstime. Each provides a different context for language use, and teachers need to consider the various speaking and listening demands and plan accordingly. Modelling should of course feature prominently in the process of introducing children to any of them.

News in pairs or groups

Moving away from the whole class newstime format to some form of grouping reduces the stress on younger children that comes from being asked to listen for too long. Small groups also offer children many more opportunities both to be news-giver and to ask questions or make comments on others' news. Some teachers provide groups with a 'talking teddy' or 'talking stick' for the speaker to hold whenever it's his or her turn to give news. Other group members ask questions and make comments before the stick or teddy is passed on to the next child.

The news group of three has built a model of a space creature and is answering questions about it from another group.

News in pairs is in some ways more akin to a structured conversation than an oral presentation, although the teacher may still want to stress the importance of letting the speaker finish before the partner asks questions or offers comment. A variant of this is to provide some telephones (either toys or obsolete ones) and create a 'news centre' as one of the morning's English activities. The presence of the telephone, even when children are sitting side by side or opposite each other, makes for a certain distance from the here and now.

Telling someone else's news

This extension of news in pairs is designed to modify the regular 'once-a-week' newstime structure. Essentially it involves one of a pair listening to the other's news and then presenting it to the whole class. Responsibilities are shared — the original speaker/news-giver must try to provide enough detail for the listener to relay (but not too much), and the listener must watch for gaps in the news that the speaker should be asked about.

News on tape

Recording news suits older children best. It can be organised from time to time as a homework activity, or a 'news desk' can be set up with a cassette recorder in the quietest corner of the classroom, or somewhere outside. Children still need to do some rehearsal before taping their news, and they can also be encouraged to emulate professional newsreaders. Topics can be set to urge them to go beyond recounts of weekend experience.

During the day class members listen individually to the taped news items, which are then discussed briefly during a sharing time at the end of the day — perhaps with some reflection on the skills of the presenters, or on what makes for an interesting news report.

The following alternatives move from oral news to a written form.

Class news book

Many teachers of younger children find value in scribing one child's news in front of the class every day, partly because it gives them an opportunity for explicit modelling of many aspects of written language. Children subsequently illustrate their own news, and the book is used during silent reading time and as a reference during writing time.

Personal diaries or journals

Often, in classes of younger children, the group who told their news on a particular day also write that news in their journals. Older children might write directly into their journals, but many teachers like to maintain an oral component by having them talk to a partner about their chosen topic before writing.

One teacher of young children begins with the writing of news and then leads through reading back to talking and listening. This is how she describes it:

> To incorporate talking, listening, reading and writing as part of newstime, I organise once a week for students to choose a partner, write their news in a news book, read it to their partner and ask questions of each other. Then they return to the class circle, where they each tell their partner's news. This gives them a purpose for writing, reading, listening to and processing information (i.e. to retell it in front of their peers). They also have a written record of their own news to keep.

Class diaries

Older children can be involved in keeping a class journal or diary — a record of the life of the class. In this book, selected children record significant class events, such as excursions, visitors to the classroom, sports days, or highlights of the day, such as an interesting science experiment or the response to the end of a serialised novel. Part of the writing experience is making a judgement about how much detail should be included for particular experiences. This can involve extensive class discussion, as can the possibilities of placing material in a school newsletter or presenting it to an assembly.

Acknowledgement

Many thanks to Anne Bergan, Cheryl Gunter, Jill Isbister, Rona Parker, Sandy Rayner and Robyn Wild for some anecdotes about their practice which have been incorporated in this chapter.

5

Newstime and oral narrative

ROBYN CUSWORTH

Narrative enables children to make meanings in language in a particularly rich, extended, complex and powerful way. (Fox 1988, p. 55)

Everyone tells stories, whether they're recounting past experiences, using an anecdote to illustrate a point of view, or constructing a fictitious tale to amuse their friends, parents or children. This chapter examines the importance of storying (or oral narrative) in our lives, and then explores whether newstime as currently conceived is providing a venue for oral narrative. The final section of the chapter includes suggestions for facilitating the development of oral narrative in K–6 classrooms.

It's widely agreed that narrative or story plays a very important role in our lives, and that the oral tradition of storying is significant in every culture. Many educators have emphasised that 'people by nature lead storied lives and tell stories of them' (Connelly & Clandinin 1990, p. 2) because, as one of the few cultural universals, stories help us define who we are. They enable us to make meaning out of experiences and are as 'necessary to us as food and shelter' (Young 1991, p. 2).

We think and dream in narrative forms. Nevertheless, Bruner (1986) argues that western cultures have overvalued the technical and scientific modes of thinking (and writing), leading to a disregard of oral storytelling and a devaluing of the conceptual role that narrative plays in our lives. Certainly it's true that oral storying often disappears from the classroom once students develop the ability to read and write.

It's also clear that oral narrative plays an extremely important role in the child's construction of self. A special significance has been attached to the oral stories of young children, which have been said to reflect their inner experiences, giving parents and teachers a window onto the child's imagination. Children use stories and the opportunity to tell them as metaphors 'to bring together in a meaningful relationship what they still need to discover and explore' (Meek 1991, p. 113). Personal stories recur frequently during their everyday play experiences, changing according to who is present during the storytelling. There is also evidence to suggest that children use storytelling to resolve traumatic experiences, and that they personalise someone else's story to meet their own needs.

Developing a sense of story

A child's sense of story is evident between eighteen months and two years, with narratives about personal experiences beginning to become a regular part of parent-child interaction from about the age of two. Studies of narrative practices in different cultural groups confirm that stories are often told with young children as co-narrators: the child will tell a story about a shared experience with another family member. Alternatively a family member will relate an incident about a child in the child's hearing and encourage his or her participation. Oral narrative practices like these are embedded in the family practices of many cultural groups and are often taken for granted.

It's equally clear that different cultural groups use oral narrative differently. Heath's (1982, 1983) study of three cultural groups in North Carolina, all living within a few kilometres of each other, exemplified this point. Whilst 'Trackton' children (from a black working-class community) were encouraged to embellish their narratives imaginatively, those from 'Roadville' (a white working-class community) were expected to relate only what had actually happened — 'the whole truth and nothing but the truth'. Children from a more middle-class background ('Maintown') were usually encouraged to do both.

A child who shares a story can be in control of its tone, content, characters and sequence of events. Often children choose to place themselves at the centre of a narrative because:

> *being a character in a story is a dominant feature of children's play in our culture.*
> *Children fictionalise themselves as they play and they create the world where the*
> *fiction allows them to explore both the world they know and the one they 'make*
> *up'. The world of images is as real as any other, rule-governed, and yet wholly at*
> *the disposal of the one who makes it.*
>
> (Meek & Mills 1988, pp. 108–09)

Thus oral narrative plays a very important role in the development of the child's imagination. Joshua's narrative, reproduced below, demonstrates the influence of fairytales on his storytelling style:

Once there was a person in town and he wanted some money. He wanted some food to eat. And he wanted a glass of milk. So he ran to the Post Office to get some money. But he didn't know where to go and he ended up in the forest. He ran till he found a cottage. And there was a witch inside so he didn't go in. And he went to another cottage. And then he ran till he was trapped and that's all.

(Joshua, 3 years and 8 months)

Joshua is, to use Carol Fox's (1988, 1993) phrase, 'talking like a book'. Children's interaction with adults and peers as they relate stories facilitates their move from an immediate and expressive use of oral language to more abstract uses of language — from talking and drawing to reading and writing. How then can oral story/narrative be described or defined?

The structure of story

Three essential phases of a story were identified by Aristotle (as reported in Hardy 1975): beginning, middle and end. In recent times genre theorists (e.g. Martin & Rothery 1982) have described these three stages more specifically. They assert that narratives are those texts which contain an Orientation, a Dilemma or Complication, a Resolution, and sometimes a Coda. However, this definition of narrative through story grammar seems too reductive because it focuses almost exclusively on plot structure located within a time frame. It does not explain the 'metaphorical dimension of storytelling' (Fox 1993, p. 71), nor will it account for the structure of Aboriginal dreamtime stories. In fact many oral narratives are not constructed in such a linear fashion, and some writers (e.g. Spender 1990) have suggested that the closure element and a sense of finality are not always necessary or desirable.

As early as 1932, Bartlett was claiming that people asked to tell a story are rarely able to do so in step-by-step fashion. Instead they tend to simplify or transform their stories over time, although the overall organisation of each story persists, partly because it's associated with affective concepts like doubt, hesitation and surprise. In reality we construct for ourselves what we choose to remember and how we remember it.

Labov's (1972) work with the oral narratives of black male adolescents, based on their personal experiences, demonstrated the importance of the storyteller's language and style in creating a narrative framework. Labov suggested that different storytelling 'competences' develop within different cultural and social frameworks, and so the opportunity to share stories apprentices children to their culture and alerts them to their own unique position within that tradition.

Alongside this appreciation of differences in children's orientation to storytelling is evidence that middle-class mainstream teachers have unwittingly tended to place more value on the kind of oral narratives they would tell themselves. Oral narratives that aren't linearly sequenced along one particular theme or story-line and lack a definitive closure have been regarded less highly. This may mean that children whose stories are less valued will lose confidence in their own narrative voice.

Using newstime to develop oral narrative

If oral narrative is a universal phenomenon, common to all cultural groups despite variations in voice, then children need opportunities to share stories. If narrative has been so important at home in helping them define themselves and develop their imaginations, it seems important that they be given opportunities to story their life once at school. This rationale may initially have led to the inclusion of 'Newstime' (a.k.a. 'Show and Tell', 'Bring and Brag', 'Sharing Time', 'Gossip' or 'Circle Time') in the early childhood and primary curricula of many western countries. Apparently it was felt that providing an occasion for children to share a personal experience or talk about a favourite belonging would both build a bridge between home and school experiences and encourage the development of oral narrative. At the same time, developing children's confidence with oral language would help prepare them for literacy development.

In the last thirty to forty years newstime has become taken for granted — so much a part of pre-schools, long day care centres and K–2 classrooms that it has been fictionalised in stories about school. For example, in Beverly Cleary's *Ramona the Pest*, when Ramona discloses to her class her doll's name (Chevrolet, after her aunt's car), she is taken aback by their laughter. And in Libby Hathorn's *Freya's Fantastic Surprise*, where Freya uses more and more unlikely newstime stories to try to gain approval from her classmates, she feels their rejection intensely.

In a recent study of K–2 teachers across New South Wales (Cusworth 1994, 1995), 92% of the 393 respondents reported that they were programming newstime daily. The time allotted ranged from 15 to 75 minutes, with most teachers allowing between 15 and 25 minutes — quite a slice of the Kindergarten day. Despite this prominence in the early childhood curriculum, however, newstime has been largely under-theorised, in some instances becoming very much an ad hoc practice.

Although the results of the study just mentioned have been reported elsewhere, a brief summary of the questionnaire findings may shed some light on teachers' current newstime practices. Respondent teachers gave a variety of reasons for programming newstime regularly; in fact seventeen distinct reasons emerged as the responses were analysed. They are listed below, with quotations from several respondents appended to each one by way of illustration.

1 Oral language skill development (*encourages oral expression; extends vocabulary skills; opportunity to speak in a public forum; allows the teacher to monitor speech and language structure; to help develop speech and enunciation in individual children; an introduction to public speaking*).

2 Self-esteem development (*they gain confidence; it is very important that children are given an opportunity for saying 'this is me', 'I am worthwhile ...'; to promote the concept that every child has something to offer*).

3 Listening skill development (*they learn to listen attentively to others; development of active listening skills; practise listening manners*).

4 Providing a link between home and school (*many spend much time before they arrive at school deciding what they want to tell; children like to talk about themselves and their families; to bond home and school*).

5 Routine/settling activity (*a good way of drawing children together as a group; routine development in learning days of the week and names of children listed for each day; a settling time; it allows spontaneous talk to have a place, thus permitting work time to be quieter*).

6 Encourages children to ask interesting questions (*develops questioning; encourages children to ask relevant questions*).

7 Facilitates the development of literacy skills (*aids their process writing; forms the basis of the reading, writing and spelling activity which follows; storywriting often results from news*).

8 Allows time for housekeeping (*can collect money and notes; if necessary to collect money, children can conduct this session with minimum supervision, frequently too I'm quickly correcting comprehension sheets*).

9 Develops a sense of community in the classroom (*children learn to value and understand others; children develop a caring attitude to their peers; gives children a sense of belonging and togetherness; to help form class into a cohesive unit in a warm and supportive environment*).

10 Enables students to share something of personal significance (*children really want/need to share/show aspects of their personal life, and so do I!*).

11 Increases students' awareness of current events (*to glean understanding of world events; halfway through Year 2 news must become real news from the newspaper, TV, etc.*).

12 Allows the teacher to get to know the children (*teacher gains under-standing of children's interests and knowledge; gives me a chance to question their home life to see if they are happy; it gives me a chance to hear of any socially significant changes in the child's life, e.g. dad's in jail or mum's having a baby*).

13 Provides a student-directed activity (*allows for children to run or control a segment of the day; the need for newstime comes from the children themselves*).

14 Encourages the development of courtesy (*children learn to take turns . . . raise hands to ask questions . . . how to speak to other children*).

15 Enjoyment (*children are enthusiastic about sharing exciting/newsworthy events with their peers; children enjoy it and are upset whenever it's missed*).

16 Controls amount of student talk time (*children want to talk and this is a controlled time for them; hopefully means that they don't need to tell their friends what they have been doing during class time*).

17 Encourages oral storytelling (*oral storytelling — ordering thoughts*).

Most respondent teachers concentrated on oral language skill develop-ment; only one cited the importance of oral narrative or storying as a reason for programming newstime every day. Implicit in this emphasis on skill development is the assumption that children need help to become competent communicators. There is, however, a good deal of research which suggests that children beginning school are already very capable conversationalists, 'with a reasonably sophisticated understanding of discourse skills' (Evans 1984, p. 130). This finding may be seen to support the claim by Collins and Michaels (1986, p. 221) that teachers expect only a 'narrow literate standard', which may lead to 'a decline in the quality and quantity of interaction'. Yet there is still much to understand about the way teachers evaluate and shape the oral language offers of their students 'on the spot' and the consequent literacy development of these students. Nevertheless, for us as educators, it is crucial not to underestimate what children can already do, just as it is crucial to find a way for children to share their stories and show them that these stories are important and valuable.

It appeared that newstime was perceived by the majority of respondent teachers as an occasion for students to engage in individual performances as a way of demonstrating their oracy skills. This was suggested by the terms teachers used to describe oral skill development in their questionnaire answers (e.g. *oral expression; vocabulary skills; opportunity to speak in a public forum; allows the teacher to monitor speech and language structure; help develop*

speech and enunciation in individual children; an introduction to public speaking).
They seemed to see newstime as a forerunner to public speaking rather than
as a venue for storytelling. Certainly the parents interviewed about their
expectations of newstime in a later phase of the study said that they hoped it
would prepare their children to talk with confidence in front of large groups
of people. The opportunity to tell a story as a valuable or worthwhile activity
in itself appeared to be scarcely recognised.

Space to tell a story?

The survey also sought to investigate how teachers organised their classes
for newstime by asking them to draw their classroom arrangement for news,
as well as describing a typical newstime activity. Their drawings suggested
that a number of traditional classroom structures were most commonly
favoured, even though these tend to inhibit interactive questioning and
student discussion. More than half the teachers showed themselves sitting
either at the front of the massed class with the newsgiver, or behind the
whole class group. Other teachers indicated that they remained removed
from the news session, sitting at their desks. The circle formation was
infrequently used, and questionnaire responses also revealed that not all
children were given the opportunity to share news each day. The table below
summarises the preferred classroom arrangements.

Set up	Frequency	Percentage
Trad.	274	69.9
Groups	9	2.3
Circle	38	9.7
Mixed	40	10.2
N/A	31	7.9
Total	**392**	**100**

Classroom arrangements for newstime

The teacher was most likely to be seated at the front of the class with
younger age groups (53.6% for Kindergarten and 55.5% for Year 1, compared with 39.3% for Year 2), perhaps reflecting a perception that younger
children need more adult input. Year 2 teachers made most use of the whole
circle formation. Some teachers used a variety of formations, incorporating
a time for a whole class plenary as well as other talk opportunities. It is clear,
however, that very few teachers set up physical structures conducive to the
kind of interactive discussion they nominated as one of their reasons for
programming a daily newstime.

Many teachers intimated a tendency to control what happened at newstime, searching for what they considered correct answers to 'sensible' questions, and restricting children's opportunities to talk by timing each newsgiver or limiting the number of questions that could be asked about a particular news item. Others wrote explicitly about using newstime to reduce the daily quantity of children's talk, reasoning that if they gave it a particular venue, other learning tasks during the day would be less prone to chatter. Given the importance of talk in learning and the crucial links between talking and thinking development discussed earlier, it is disheartening that teachers still express the need to control children's talk-time during learning activities which are explicitly intended to provide a venue for them to talk.

'Show-and-Tell' rather than storytelling

A recent study by Barbara Kamler of the experiences of children during their first month at school, and the processes by which they absorb gendered relationships, included an examination of 'Morning Talk' in a suburban Prep classroom in Victoria. Kamler (1994, p. 4) found that the items brought in during the first four weeks of school were 'strongly gendered'. Girls brought more dolls and soft toys, while boys usually brought objects like cars. The study included a particular focus on the teacher's talk when girls displayed dolls, which revealed that she 'unwittingly produced gendered texts that positioned herself and the girls in marginal ways', despite her usually exemplary work for gender equity. She equated doll behaviour with good schoolgirl behaviour, and the attributes of the doll being displayed were confused with the attributes of the doll's owner.

It's clear that a newstime situation similar to this and based on 'Show-and-Tell' has a very different interaction structure to a situation in which children are encouraged to share a past or projected experience. The patterning of talk in a show-and-tell situation would seem to discourage oral narrative — at least initially — as the 'shower-and-teller' is likely to be limited to a set role while the special object is displayed. The foregrounding of objects also communicates implicit messages about possessing them. Certainly it poses a real problem for a child not able to bring something 'new' each week on his or her designated newsday. I well remember my own children begging me to buy a new toy so that they would have something extra special to talk about. Furthermore, the use of language in this type of news session is highly dependent on the object being displayed (an ancillary use [Halliday 1985] as compared with a constitutive use, which is less dependent on a specific object or happening) and seems to contradict the perception of newstime as a venue for learning to 'talk like a book'.

Making more of newstime: implications for classrooms

Newstime, then, needs to be seen as an opportunity within the curriculum for children to share personal stories — not simply to develop self-esteem or oral language skills, but also to make sense of their world and their place within it. Yet children need more than just a venue to share their personal narratives; they need to have them accepted, even honoured, by others. The children in Kindergarten who were interviewed about newstime in Cusworth's study said that they liked it because they wanted a space in their day when others listened to *them*. It's also interesting to note that in transcripts of newstime recorded by Kindergarten teachers, children often raised life problems. They wanted to discuss philosophical issues concerned with death and injury, or moving to another city or town. However, the teachers often found such issues difficult to handle and immediately changed the topic.

Karen Gallas has documented the story of one six-year-old child's journey in storying over a year of class sharing time. At the beginning of the year the child, Jiana, who had experienced a great deal of family trauma, could barely talk. In fact 'she couldn't collect her thoughts clearly enough to get them out in a coherent way' (Gallas 1992, p. 174), but she was keen to participate in sharing time. The other children 'drew her out' until she no longer needed to use objects to talk about but instead shared her family's problems

Never forget what an important part gossip plays in classroom life.

with the group. Although some of these problems had been traumatic for the family, Gallas notes that Jiana 'wasn't ashamed. She was just telling her story'. The interesting thing at this point is that her language had by now become well structured and coherent.

Sharing times in this classroom next moved on to imaginative stories, and it was Jiana who initiated the change. Through the sharing of these fictional narratives, other children in the class were able 'to engage in a new way of talking' (p. 181). Some of the children who were very skilled in the traditional, more formulaic sharing times felt challenged to begin with, but Gallas concludes that:

> The fictional stories expanded the children's ability to speak about the more subterranean issues of the community: about belonging and inclusion, about unspoken wishes to overcome barriers . . . (p. 181)

The development of Jiana's oracy, coupled with her introduction of fictional narratives to the classroom, provides very powerful evidence for the value of a newstime which is about storying rather than technical routine.

So . . . how do we make the most of newstime?

1 Examine existing practice

First of all, the rituals which are part of any newstime (and which we often establish unthinkingly) need to be examined to ensure that the messages they carry are consistent with our purposes as teachers. For example:

- When children are allocated a particular day to share their news, it may create undue tension if a designated newsgiver does not have an appropriate item to share.
- If newsgivers always relate their stories to the whole class, wriggling and restlessness are inevitable.
- If children are forced to sit 'en masse' facing the newsgiver at the front of the room, how will they be able to interact with each other's stories?
- Is the emphasis on bringing an object necessary?
- Can children be encouraged to talk about things that have happened or things they have made, rather than things they own?
- If the teacher is not involved in newstime at all but uses it for administration or marking, what message is being conveyed to the newsgivers?

2 Consider group activities

As mentioned above, only 2.3% of the teachers surveyed by Cusworth used 'buzz groups' or pairs in their newstime. Providing opportunities for children to share a story with a small group or a partner can be a useful starting point for developing confidence and thinking through how a story is staged or sequenced. Setting guidelines (e.g. *Tomorrow we're going to talk about a time when we were frightened*) can also be helpful. Give children the freedom to use their imaginations — do stories always have to be an exact account of what really happened, or will you allow a little storyteller's licence?

Developing children's ability to actively listen to each other during these times can be furthered by asking listeners to relate the story they heard to someone else, or even to draw or map the important parts of the story as they heard it.

3 Incorporate shared story sessions

There are a number of storytelling games that can be played in whole group circle sessions to encourage children to share stories. For example, taking a well-known fairytale as a base and jointly constructing a story can be lots of fun. Children can be encouraged to add details and think specifically about character and description and the story's purpose, as well as the plot sequence. They can examine how the story is structured and compare it with other story genres to find common and different features. An excursion or similar shared activity can be treated in the same way.

Delight in hearing stories recorded by other classmates is very evident here.

4 Honouring stories

Taping stories, illustrating them or acting as a scribe to document them are all ways of confirming the importance of the oral narratives that children tell.

5 Share your purposes with students and parents

Parents need to understand what your purposes are and that you're not wasting time. So do your students. Where does their perception that real school work is only related to writing come from? We need to spend time sharing our ideas and getting across why talk in general and, more particularly, oral narrative are important in the development of a child's learning and thinking.

Conclusion

Confidence gained with oral narrative during newstime can enhance children's thinking and imaginative development and help them define their sense of self. As teachers we need to establish a classroom context where children feel that their own experiences are worth sharing with other class members. Newstime must offer opportunities to share stories, either real or imagined, in small groups as well as with the whole class. We also need to provide time for real talk about issues that concern our students, and we need to model active listening instead of giving absent-minded responses. Most importantly, we have to find a way of communicating our conviction that oral narrative is just as important as the written form, that talk is as valuable as writing, and that time spent in oral storying will help us determine who we are.

6

Cooperative learning: enhancing talking and listening

KATHY CREE

SANDRA DONALDSON

The background

We become interested in cooperative learning several years ago when we took an opportunity to join in an action research project. At the time we were team teaching and finding ourselves concerned about the disruptive behaviour of some of our students. The project aimed to deal with such difficulties by encouraging cooperative learning. By the time it came to an end, we had decided that this kind of learning had a lot to offer students as well as teachers.

Thus our initial concern with the management of a few students led to the adoption of strategies that enhanced classroom learning for everybody. In certain lessons we were able to shift the focus from teacher-centred learning to student-centred learning. Students developed skills which enabled them to be responsible not only for managing groups but the resources involved and evaluation of the activity. They became independent learners, assisting each other, discussing ideas and information, and incidentally supplying a range of models of behaviour and language use. When all the students were surveyed, girls in particular nominated this type of learning as their preferred style.

Our learning process

Introducing cooperative learning structures has taught us many things. We've realised that we need to be more imaginative in designing tasks, so that cooperative learning principles can be embedded in the units of work we plan. To help us do this, we've attended professional development courses, both as participants and speakers, and have found that the spirit of cooperative learning is reflected in the way in which ideas are willingly shared among teachers. Such collegiality is vital for us if we're to continue to be creative.

We have also drawn on a variety of sources for developing our practice. Many useful strategies can be derived from social skills programs, and there are several texts available which provide ideas for teaching the skills required for effective group work.

Although we're now a number of years on from the initial project and teach in different schools, we both continue to use cooperative learning as the core of our classroom management. Of course there are moments of strong teacher direction when we need to make points about content, language or behaviour, but we believe that the most effective classrooms are those in which students are frequently engaged in productive group work and encouraged to take responsibility for the processes of learning. So in the following pages we:

- describe how to begin using cooperative learning strategies
- discuss some of the skills students need
- detail some practical ways of incorporating the techniques into learning in various key learning areas.

Getting started with a buddy system

In our rooms we operate a buddy system. Sandra picked up the idea from an inservice where another teacher, Maxine Green, spoke about her classroom organisation. The buddy system has enabled us to model and develop many of the interpersonal skills required for effective group work. It also provides students with opportunities to develop relationships of mutual respect and care for those outside their immediate friendship group.

The basis of the system is that every fortnight students take a new partner, though their choice is usually 'random'. Teachers find many different ways of organising this — below are two that have worked for us.

Matching games

The teacher distributes interestingly shaped cards cut in half. Students move around the room looking for their 'other half'. The first pair of students to find a match checks it with the teacher, and if it's correct, they select their desk for the fortnight. Other means of match-making include card sets with factors and their corresponding products, synonyms and antonyms, and words misspelt and correctly spelt.

A movement game

This game begins with half the class forming a circle. The other half forms another by standing opposite someone in the inner circle. Then all the students turn round so that they're no longer facing each other. Both circles move on four places in opposite directions, and the students turn to face their new partners.

Working with buddies

Buddy tasks can be as few or as numerous as you wish. We usually start the fortnight by encouraging pairs simply to talk and find out things about each other's family, friends, likes and dislikes. They can then report to a group or the whole class something they've learnt about their partner.

We often encourage students to work in buddy pairs during routine classroom activities (e.g. learning spelling and tables, drafting and editing

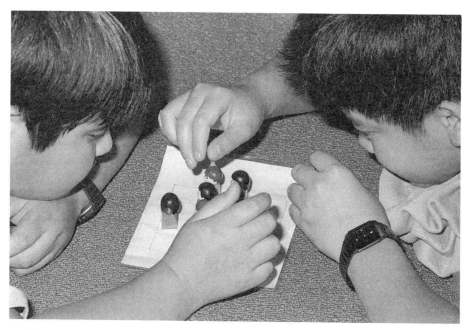

Working in pairs is one way for children to develop and practice skills for larger group activities. These boys are solving a maths problem together, talking continually as they do so.

written texts, or working out cloze passages). Once the task has been completed, buddies can join another pair to compare their work, offer advice and make changes if necessary.

The social advantages of the buddy system are many. Because of the random nature of the pairing process and because partners are changed frequently, students are able to work in combinations that probably wouldn't happen otherwise. Girls and boys frequently find themselves working together (which they might not choose to do normally), and this is an important step towards establishing positive working relationships within the classroom and beyond. Students from different language backgrounds, students from the same language background and students with varying degrees of English language proficiency are all able to interact.

Social skills for cooperative learning

The buddy system is an excellent introduction to the social skills required for successful group work. Here we should emphasise that such skills do need to be taught — we use role plays, games and activities to make them quite obvious to our students. Important skills discussed below include the use of positive talk or 'build-ups', listening, turn-taking, participation, 'brave talk' and observation.

Positive talk

We feel that the use of positive or encouraging talk is one of the most important skills we can teach to students. After all, it's very easy for class members to fall into a pattern of criticising others' mistakes, or their contributions to whole class or group work, which often has the effect of inhibiting individuals to a serious extent. To counteract this tendency, it's necessary to create a positive classroom atmosphere in which all students feel that their contributions will be accepted and valued.

Positive talk can be broken down into three separate steps: viz. making contact (often with the eyes), using a calm voice, and making positive comments. The basic idea can be introduced with a game like this. Take a piece of paper and ask students to imagine that it represents an individual's feelings; then invite them to offer comments that are hurtful or belittling. Alternatively, stage a role play of a hurtful incident or, in the early years, use puppets. As each hurtful comment is given, tear a strip off the paper, explaining that this demonstrates how damaging negative talk is. Follow up with a discussion about encouraging talk, and then ask students to contribute some positive comments. With each comment, reconstruct the torn piece of paper to show how powerful this kind of talk can be

It's a good idea to make charts to help reinforce the use of positive talk. A 'Y' chart shows what it looks like, sounds like and feels like:

Feels like
important   useful
valued   good
trusted

Looks like	Sounds like
facing the speaker	mm
eye contact	yes
nodding	oh
leaning in	uh huh
smiles	why
gestures	yeah

A 'T' chart shows what it looks like and sounds like:

Looks like	Sounds like
facing the speaker	mm
eye contact	yes
nodding	oh
leaning in	uh huh
smiles	why
gestures	yeah

Displaying a list of build-ups in the classroom has the same reinforcing effect. You can ask each child to contribute one written on coloured card, and perhaps decorated. Examples include *Great try, Well done, Way to go, Mad, Neat, Clever thinking, Amazing* and *Fantastic effort*. The list serves as a reference for the class as they go about their daily activities, as well as in group time.

Another idea to reinforce the use of positive talk is to give all students envelopes on which they stick a photograph of themselves. These are then placed on a board, with a box of coloured strips of paper and textas nearby. Each time a student gives a positive comment to another, the recipient writes it down and puts the strip in the giver's envelope. Once a week comments are shared and tallied.

With younger children, a name chart may be a more suitable alternative. As a child receives a positive comment, he or she puts a stamp or dot beside the name of the child who made the comment. Then everyone can easily see who is using encouraging talk.

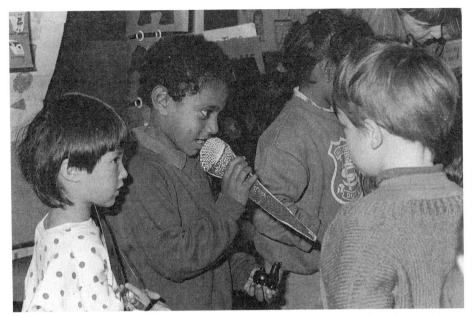

Using the 'microphone' helps this young child assume the role of speaker and at the same time underscores the listening roles of the other children.

Listening, participation and turn-taking skills

It's crucial for students to have well-established listening skills if they are to participate fully in group activities. During group sessions they will be called upon to listen, take turns and comment on others' ideas. The act of listening can be made explicit by encouraging them to follow these three steps:

Stop (stop what you're doing and stay still)

Look (turn your head to the speaker)

Listen (think about what the speaker is saying).

One way of establishing a routine whereby students take turns in talking and listening to each other, either in paired or group work, is to use a speaking piece. A cube or ball left in the centre of each group works well, and one of our colleagues uses toy microphones with her junior class. Students hold the ball (or whatever it is) either when it's their turn to speak or when they have something to say, and others in the group must listen. If it so happens that one student is having too many turns at the expense of others, then some limits have to be imposed.

A variation on the single speaking piece is for students in a group to each have a box of cubes or blocks and place one in the centre every time they contribute an idea. If a student has used up all his or her blocks, it's time to listen. If, on the other hand, a student uses none or very few, then he or she needs encouraging to contribute more to the group's discussion.

Brave talk

There's often a need for explicit teaching about effective ways of communicating assertively in group work. When students complain that they haven't had their turn, or that they've been intimidated in expressing divergent opinions, it's best to teach them how to use 'brave talk' to try and negotiate these difficulties for themselves. It's a skill that students can learn by following these steps:

1 Ask yourself whether it's the appropriate time to be assertive (i.e. have you tried to contribute in the normal way?).

2 Make contact (whether with eyes, gesture or touch) and put on a brave look.

3 Use a calm, brave voice to deliver your message to your audience.

Role plays are the most effective way of teaching this skill and generating discussion about appropriate times to exercise it. You'll also need to teach the difference between a normal and an assertive voice, so that all students understand and can use both. As a reinforcement, 'Y' and 'T' charts can be made to answer the question *What does brave talk look like, sound like and feel like when you use it?*

Observation

This involves asking one group member to take on the role of observer to see whether the rest of the group is staying on task. The observer can also reflect on why things work and why they sometimes don't go as planned. Role plays are useful for demonstrating the necessary skills (e.g. being clear about the task, listening, watching and note-taking), and students can join in making charts to record the qualities of a good observer.

In the middle and upper primary years, you might provide a proforma identifying students in the group and the skills necessary for completing a particular task successfully, with some additional space for a comment on group performance. A sheet like this provides a scaffold for the observer's report. Younger children can use a pictorial checklist to tick off who's using build-ups, taking turns or listening carefully.

Students should of course take turns at being the observer: they really enjoy the role because they're in control and can make judgments (in a positive way) about how others are performing. They also become increasingly capable of reflecting on their own behaviour in groups.

Explicit teaching of cooperative learning skills

When we teach these skills, our lessons follow this kind of sequence:

1 Games to reinforce each skill at the opening and close of each lesson.

2 Constructing 'Y' or 'T' charts to show what each skill looks like and sounds like to the recipient and feels like for the giver.

3 Activities designed to employ the particular skill being developed.

Lack of space prevents us including examples of the games and activities here. However, many are to be found in Susan Hill's book *Games That Work*, where they are clustered under appropriate headings (e.g. listening skill games, eye contact games, turn-taking games, talking games, group work games and name games).

Students particularly enjoy this part of the program and quickly become aware of the skills we want them to acquire — skills that are vital if they are going to talk and listen purposefully in lessons where we use cooperative learning groups as a major teaching strategy across all KLAs.

Roles for use in cooperative learning

After covering the social skills described above, we introduce students to the different roles group members can take in cooperative learning. Needless to say, not all roles need be used in all lessons; some tasks might be suited to two roles, some might demand more. When not in a particular role, students remain active as participants in the group. Possible roles include:

encourager – uses positive talk

recorder – takes down necessary information for the group

materials manager – gets appropriate materials and returns them after use

observer – notes who's on task and what students are doing and saying

reporter – presents the group's findings to the class/teacher

checker – makes sure every member understands what the group findings are

timekeeper – keeps an eye on the time limit for the task and ensures that things are finished on time.

These terms can of course be modified to suit different ages and stages of development. Many teachers make badges to identify different roles within groups.

Sometimes when we're forming groups we use the same random, game-like approach as we do for pairing buddies. This ensures that the groups are of mixed gender, language background and ability. Groups can be of course be constituted in other ways (e.g. by interest, friendship or ability) to suit particular circumstances. Nevertheless we prefer mixed groups.

Linking cooperative learning to de Bono's 'thinking hats'

Why teach thinking skills?

Soon after we began using cooperative learning, we noticed problems when students were required to develop a group idea or product. They seemed to become fixated on their own ideas and couldn't see the advantages or disadvantages of the range of ideas presented by the group. Contributions and discussion became stifled. Clearly they had to be encouraged to think in different ways to solve problems and to generate and accept ideas, and so we introduced the 'Thinking Hats' program (de Bono 1985). The cooperative learning skills already established provided a structure for learning to use thinking skills.

When we're teaching thinking skills, we first of all demonstrate the six types of thinking and then encourage students to use them in joint practice sessions. Subsequently we expect individuals to use them with increasing autonomy. Different coloured hats symbolise the different types of thinking, and although the hats are really metaphors, in the early stages they can be realised as objects to give students a visual signal that a particular type of thinking is to be used.

The six thinking hats

Yellow hat thinking is concerned with the strengths of particular ideas or texts. We find that when students join us in looking purposefully and deliberately at the opportunities presented by different situations, they learn to suspend judgement and share a wider range of possible responses. We use this approach in a range of curriculum areas: for example, with literary texts (*What worked well in this poem?*), or when students are learning to write arguments. The result is that when discussing a particular topic or issue, they come to look for its positive qualities together.

Purple hat thinking is concerned with looking for disadvantages or potential difficulties. It may involve asking why something doesn't work, or thinking about possible dangers. It's also useful for anticipating objections to a particular line of argument. It usually follows yellow hat thinking, when we're assessing ideas and trying to make improvements. For instance, with a poem we might go on to ask *What are the weaknesses here?* This type of thinking is often a prelude to green hat thinking.

Green hat thinking is concerned with creativity — with generating new ideas or looking for solutions, explanations and possibilities. We might use it when we're trying to explain why a character in a literary text behaves in a certain way, or when considering the range of options available to us for informing others about significant school events.

White hat thinking is concerned with looking for facts, finding information and asking questions. It's used quite extensively across curriculum areas.

We encourage students to follow these steps:

- *What do I know about this situation or problem?*
- *What do I need to know?*
- *Where can I find what I need?*

Red hat thinking is concerned with feelings (de Bono says that feeling is a type of thinking, and of course he's right). To draw attention to this sort of thinking we ask, *What hunches or intuitions do you have about this?*, *What's your opinion?*, *What do you like or dislike about this?* or *How does it make you feel?* There's no compulsion to clarify the feeling; rather we encourage students to recognise that this is the way they feel about an issue at a particular moment, that their feelings may differ from other people's, and that they may well change with more information.

As part of learning to control and use feelings in productive ways, we think it's important that they are acknowledged (without necessarily being justified or explained) in this formal and structured way. We encourage red hat thinking by proposing scenarios — for example:

Your best friend gives you a present for no reason at all. How do you feel?

Sport is cancelled. How do you feel?

We also find it useful when we're encouraging students to respond to texts — for example:

How does this TV advertisement make you feel about the product?

Sometimes we ask students to take a character's place in a certain situation (fictitious or real) and say how they feel.

Blue hat thinking is concerned with 'thinking about thinking' and is taught last. It's the control hat, used to define goals and plan how to achieve them. It's also used for continuous assessment of progress. We encourage students to remember it at all stages of the thinking process, asking themselves such questions as:

What thinking plan do I need to find and present information about the water cycle?

What is my times-table goal for this week? How can I achieve it? . . . Did the plan work?

Wearing the hats

While our aim is to develop students' abilities to use these thinking skills independently, we do spend time working on identical tasks during joint practice sessions. Students work in groups, with each group member using the same coloured hat/type of thinking at any one time. After a while they become able use the skills in sequence, depending on the goal to be achieved. The focus on thinking skills gives them clear guidelines about the sort of contributions they may individually make to a group. They also learn how to listen actively to the range of ideas presented and build on each other's suggestions.

Here's an example of the thinking hats at work. A group of upper primary students has been asked to assess a proposal that playground areas and activities should be rostered on a class basis.

1 In groups, students put on the white hat and ask questions about how the roster would operate in order to clarify what might be involved.

2 They use the yellow hat to look for positive elements in the proposal.

3 They change to the purple hat and look for weaknesses and disadvantages.

4 They put on the red hat to say how they feel about the idea.

5 Finally they put on the blue hat to summarise their group's conclusions.

Some practical uses of cooperative learning

Once students have gone some way towards assimilating the social skills, roles and ways of thinking involved in cooperative learning, classroom applications are limitless. The examples which follow aren't startlingly new, but cooperative learning techniques can enhance the opportunities they offer for speaking and listening.

1001 Questions

We've used this game (also known as Enquiry and Elimination) with a variety of curriculum topics. Here we've chosen one from the Science and Technology area, where students had been building their knowledge of the appearance and behaviour of sea animals, as well as exploring animal taxonomies. The transcript below demonstrates how the game requires students to draw on their background knowledge of a topic and gives them opportunities to reuse the associated technical vocabulary.

The background to the transcript can be given fairly quickly. Four students, Benita, Ken, Vishnay and Neil, are seated around a number of cut-out pictures of marine animals. Vishnay is 'in' and has secretly selected one animal. The task for the rest of the group is to determine which he's chosen, asking as few questions as possible. The questions must be thoughtful and allow initially for the elimination of more than one animal.

The easiest way to comment on someone else's work is to talk about it; these girls are helping each other with whale diagrams from another stage of the Sea Animals unit.

Vishnay can only answer *yes* or *no*. Once the three students have established which phylum (vertebrates or invertebrates) they are looking for, they turn unwanted pictures face-down. They then ask about particular class characteristics (e.g. *Is it a fish? Does it have fins?*). Turn-taking is facilitated by the passing of a microphone, and we often suggest that students let it go round the circle at least twice before they ask any questions about specific creatures.

The transcript records Vishnay having trouble classifying the animal; Benita helps him.

N: Is your creature . . . a . . . vertebrate, sorry, a vertebrate?

V: *(tentatively)* Uh . . . no.

K: It's invertebrate.

B: However, let's turn them round *(begins turning over the pictures of vertebrates)*.

N: No.

V: No, it's not a vertebrate.

B: OK, an invertebrate is one that doesn't have a backbone. Does it have a shell? *(V shakes head)* Turn them over.

V: Oh yes! It is a vertebrate!

B: It is?

K: Oh no. *(Pause while students rearrange the pictures to start again)*

N: Is it dangerous?

V: Sort of.

B: Is it a fish? A fish with fins?

K: This fish? *(points to one)*

V: Can't guess.

B: *(to K)* You're guessing it . . . Has it got fins?

V: Yes.

B: 'Cos fish have fins.

Throughout the game the four students were encouraged to consult various charts, diagrams and lists of descriptive words available in the classroom to help them plan and frame specific questions. We use activities like this to build and reinforce the field knowledge required to write successful information reports.

Group writing

Our students often work cooperatively in writing lessons. There are opportunities for group activities throughout the writing cycle, from introducing the field through to independent construction (see Derewianka 1990, pp. 6–9).

Recently, as part of an investigation of vision, one class dissected a bullock's eye provided by the local butcher. Using their observation skills, students described and labelled the parts of the eye. Each group then produced 'outsize' diagrams and jointly constructed labels and captions for them. During this process they were able to remind each other of items and vocabulary from the original dissection. The labels and captions were then shared and edited by the whole class, and the diagrams became the starting point for further reading and writing of sustained explanatory texts about how sight works. Before producing written texts individually, students were encouraged to rehearse orally in their groups the sequence of steps in an explanation.

Group activities can also be used to explore understandings of text and grammar. Our students frequently work in groups of two or three to 'unjumble' texts and label structures typical of particular text types. Here the think/pair/share/square organisation can be useful. For example, when the class is examining procedural texts, a pair of students might be given a procedural text from a certain field (e.g. cooking) and be asked to locate the material processes (i.e. action verbs). They then join with another pair who have done the same with a text from a different area (e.g. building). In the 'square' they are able to make connections between vocabulary and topic, as well as noting the forward position of processes in this type of text.

Raps, rhymes and poetry

Cooperative learning is an ideal way to encourage the delivery of raps and rhymes in a variety of different spoken styles. Groups take away their given verse, rap or rhyme on a sheet of paper or a tape. They listen to it, say it and play with it, perhaps using body percussion, mime or actions. Then, in turn, group members put forward their ideas (no 'put-downs' allowed) before making a joint decision about the way they would like to present their text to the class.

Conclusion

Teachers often embark on programs of work that promise their students enhanced outcomes in talking and listening, and they are sometimes disappointed. However, both of us are confident that the explicit teaching of social and thinking skills described in this chapter will make talking and listening in group work more purposeful and productive, and the outcomes more nearly achievable. We see cooperative learning strategies as important steps on the way to giving students access to the language of interaction, opening up for them paths of communication that are vital for working and thinking together in positive ways. The processes take time and patience to establish, but the results are well worth the effort.

7

Towards meeting the needs of Aboriginal learners

In this chapter three teachers of Aboriginal children in different settings discuss aspects of classroom practice which enhance their oral language and literacy programs. Lesley Mills raises issues bearing on cross-cultural communication patterns, Penni Brydon describes effective strategies for the beginning years, and Kathleen Rushton details some of the ways she uses children's oral language to facilitate the development of literacy skills. Many of the strategies described suit non-Aboriginal students equally well.

Cross-cultural issues in oral language programs

LESLEY MILLS

Aboriginal English has all too often been labelled as 'bad English', 'incorrect English' or 'lazy English'. In fact, it is a recognised dialect and our Aboriginal children come to school fluent and articulate in it. They have mastered a difficult cognitive process and see themselves as successful communicators. At school, however, many find the formalities and language of the classroom quite foreign and inhibiting.

As teachers of Aboriginal students, it's our responsibility to build on the competencies they bring to school. We need to develop a comfortable environment where they feel secure enough to express themselves and take risks. We need to show them that both Aboriginal English and Standard

English are used, respected and valued, and help them to become bidialectal by teaching appropriate uses of Standard English in context.

Communication styles

[The] important challenge that you face is to understand the ways of communicating used by the Aboriginal children in your classroom. Do not judge the intelligence, cooperation, or manners of Aboriginal children in terms of mainstream culturally-biased norms, such as how to avoid silence, when to make eye contact and how to respond to questions. Recognising such cultural difference in communication is an important first step before you can teach the children to be bicultural and bidialectal and to participate in the wider Australian society.

(Eades 1995)

Body language and non-verbal cues are an integral part of Aboriginal English — as important as the spoken word — and teachers need to be honest and sincere in their interactions with Aboriginal children. They should also make time to have informal chats; Aboriginal children are always keen to talk about home and family, and if teachers show a genuine interest, they will gain valuable insights into their students' oral language skills.

In Aboriginal communities children tend to learn by observation and practice rather than through questioning and explanation. Direct questions are often considered rude; it's more usual to wait for information to be volunteered, and so silences are customary in conversation. As the avoidance of direct questioning is unusual in school contexts, Aboriginal children may be thought to be uninterested, shy or even rude. A silence can also be misunderstood by those unfamiliar with Aboriginal conventions: children may begin a response with a silence or use silence as part of a response. With this in mind, teachers must be careful not to interrupt in case children become discouraged and less secure.

Nevertheless, to succeed at school, Aboriginal children need to feel comfortable with the practice of direct questioning. Question-answer activities in all forms are invaluable here, and the children find them enjoyable and non-threatening. Hot Seat, described on p. 22, is one of a number that can be adapted for use in any curriculum area: other examples are Twenty Questions and Celebrity Heads. Twenty Questions, which is similar to 1001 Questions (pp. 76–78), begins with one child thinking of an object. The other children must try and find out what the object is by asking no more than twenty questions, which can only be answered with a *yes* or *no*. In Celebrity Heads, a well-known name is chosen and displayed so that everyone but the child who is 'in' can see it. He or she then asks questions of the others in an effort to identify the celebrity. Again the others can only answer *yes* or *no*.

Children should be assured that they are welcome to stop and ask for clarification in any situation, and their questions should be welcomed as positive signs of engagement. Many children who lack the confidence to ask questions are also 'shamed' (i.e. too shy) to ask for support in doing so, thus compounding their confusion.

When focusing on oral language skills, I find that initially children need to be immersed in informal activities which encourage discussion and cooperation across the curriculum. I favour small groups because they're much less threatening and so more likely to make children feel free to express themselves. Acting as facilitator, I move between groups to encourage and guide the oral language, at the same time assessing the capabilities of individual children in an informal situation. However, I always try to ensure that my role is limited to participation and that I avoid dominating the activity.

I attempt to involve children at every level in the development of my oral language program through the following strategies:

- explaining the reasons for having an oral language program and how it can help them as learners
- brainstorming charts which state what makes good speakers and good listeners
- developing frameworks for children to refer to when they're engaged in spoken language activities (e.g. *What? When? Where? Who? Why?*)
- providing demonstrations and modelling of a variety of spoken texts.

The content

Aboriginal children are no different from any others in that they have a great chance of success if their education is culturally relevant and interesting and respects their opinions and attitudes. The use of Aboriginal studies material (traditional or contemporary) is one way to ensure that topics will be meaningful and of interest to them. The development of poems and discussion around popular Aboriginal vernacular (as in *deadly* for *excellent* or *awesome*) can be inspirational for them, as can responses to local community speakers or issues.

Otitis media

A key issue in any discussion about language learning and Aboriginal children is Otitis media — a general term for middle-ear disease. A very common form is 'glue ear' or Otitis media with effusion. The disease is associated with colds, flu, asthma and chest infections; inflammation contributes to a build-up of fluid in the middle ear, reducing a child's capacity to hear. This is called a conductive hearing loss, because sound waves are not conducted to the inner ear and brain. The loss varies in severity and may fluctuate over time, and so it can be quite difficult to detect.

Most children have at least one episode of Otitis media before the age of five. However, it's estimated that as many as eight out of ten Aboriginal school students suffer from middle-ear infections and associated hearing loss at some time during the school year (Board of Studies NSW 1994, p. 2). Treatments such as antibiotics and surgery are used, but the disease can be difficult to diagnose early as children may have it without complaining of pain. Recurrent bouts bring the danger of permanent damage to the ear.

It's hardly surprising that these hearing difficulties, while essentially medical problems, have a profound effect on children's learning and behaviour. As teachers we know the importance of being able to hear the sounds of words in developing particular reading and spelling skills, as well as in oral vocabulary and syntactic development. It's likely that children with conductive hearing loss will have difficulty with a range of spoken language skills, such as:

- comprehension and recall of spoken information
- sustaining interactions with teachers and other students
- auditory perception and processing (e.g. hearing low intensity sounds, discriminating phonemes)
- articulating words and connected speech
- development of sound/syllable segmentation and blending.

Such difficulties in communication are exacerbated for Aboriginal children by the impact of cultural differences. When they're struggling to distinguish sounds in Standard Australian English, they may lack understandings of the context of culture or situation that will allow them to make compensating predictions or guesses. For this reason alone, teachers should endeavour to include both first and second languages and dialects in their oral language programs.

It's vital that teachers of Aboriginal children are informed about Otitis media and its implications for educational outcomes. Support and advice are available in the form of expertise provided by local and regional Aboriginal Education Consultative Groups (AECG) and specialist staff appointed to schools. Various education systems have developed support materials as well: these include processes for identifying hearing impaired students as well as strategies for enhancing their classroom learning, such as those displayed in Fig. 7.1.

Strategies for reducing noise in the classroom
- Use soft furnishings, carpet and cushions to absorb sound.
- Take account of activities in surrounding classrooms and outside so that children don't have to compete with extraneous noise.
- Encourage children to limit excess noise.

Strategies to use with the children
- Notice which children have ear problems and keep them close to you.
- Encourage active involvement and interaction.
- Keep the distance between you and the children as small as possible.
- Check that children can see your face when you're talking.
- Encourage good listening habits, such as being quiet and facing the speaker.

Strategies to enhance your teaching style
- Use visual aids as much as possible.
- Note key points on the board.
- Allow plenty of modelling and demonstration so that children can see what's required.
- Check children's understandings regularly.
- Establish clear routines.
- Make instructions and topic changes clear.

(based on Board of Studies NSW 1994, pp. 43–45)

FIG. 7.1. STRATEGIES TO ASSIST STUDENTS WITH IMPAIRED HEARING

Oral language strategies with Aboriginal children

PENNI BRYDON

Since most of my teaching experience has been with K–2 pupils, what I have to say is most immediately relevant to children in their first three years of school. None the less competent teachers will be able to adapt the strategies to meet their individual school and class needs.

Easing the transition to school

For all children (Aboriginal and non-Aboriginal) the home situation is quite different from school. There are rarely more than four or five people to communicate with and a child can usually get at least one person's attention. Pre-schools and child-care centres have quite a low child/adult ratio too, but at school children find that they're suddenly competing with twenty or more others for one adult's attention. Many find this difficult to cope with, and when the change is compounded by differences in culture and language, beginning school can be quite traumatic.

Placing children in appropriate situations is not pandering to their demands; it is meeting their needs as learners. I think it's important that wherever possible Aboriginal children are placed with a friend or relative in the same class. Yes, they will talk to each other, but this is less disruptive than having an unhappy child. One little boy who had cried almost all day stopped as soon as he was put into a class with his cousin. Whilst he would probably have stopped crying eventually, his first experience of school would have been negative, and in the long term his learning experiences and attendance patterns may have been affected.

Teachers as active listeners

The most important strategy teachers can use to encourage Aboriginal children to take part in oral language activities is to *listen*. However, it's probably one of the hardest strategies to carry through because, as teachers, we have a tendency to interrupt and correct whenever we hear inappropriate or grammatically incorrect language. Nevertheless if we stop and listen, show genuine interest and ask the right questions, our reward will be confident children who feel that they can make a positive contribution to class discussions.

Observe and listen to the children in the playground or during free play sessions. It'll soon become evident that they have lots to say, are easily understood and are confident in what they're doing. It's a good time to gain trust and build up a rapport. But if we aren't genuine, the children will see through us; they'll realise that we're only talking to them out of politeness, or for some other unknown reason, and they'll clam up. This is where the importance of listening comes in.

Once a message has been heard and we understand the basics, we can ask some pertinent questions. But we shouldn't interrupt or ask questions that have already been answered. For instance, if the conversation has been about going to a cousin's place and riding bikes, don't ask *Where did you go?* Rather phrase questions to elicit more information: for example, *Does your cousin live nearby?* (if the family isn't familiar) or *How did you get there, does it take long?* By asking for more information, we are showing our interest.

Getting ideas heard

Building up a good rapport with children in informal situations like this puts us in a better position to elicit discussion in the classroom. There, however, the restrictions of room and class sizes can still inhibit conversation, and children are expected to listen and take turns in speaking. Yet young children in particular are often bursting with important things to tell us and find it difficult not to interrupt. Generally brainstorming works well as a solution, provided that the children have some basic rules to follow — like this:

> *We're going to talk about frogs. I want you to think of all the things you know about frogs and tell me them, and I'm going to write them down. But I have to look at my writing, so I can't watch to see who has their hand up. You can call out instead of putting up your hand, but you must wait till the person speaking has finished before you start. This is called 'brainstorming', and it's a good way to get our ideas down quickly.*

Once children understand the rules and get into practice, they have no difficulty switching between brainstorming and the more regular *Hands up if you know the answer!* Brainstorming can be used for a variety of lists: for example, sad or funny things in a story, word banks, knowledge banks — even number facts.

Listening doesn't always mean being quiet

If you've ever visited a pre-school or child-care centre with a story book or big book, you'll have noticed how children call out comments about the illustrations and ask questions throughout the story. Too often though, when they come to school, all this is squashed by something like *Not now, we'll talk about it after the story's finished.* And when the story is finished, every comment and question has been forgotten because the children were so busy trying to sit still and be quiet. Expect a lot of interactions over books.

In any case, 'being quiet' isn't a reliable indicator of listening — adults have no problem thinking about other things when they're 'listening' to a boring lecture (though the speaker isn't always aware of their inattention). This makes it all the more important to teach children what listening is about. Construct a chart showing what good listeners do — but do it with the children, not for them. They'll take more notice if they feel it's 'theirs'.

Eliciting spoken language

Although there's currently a lot of emphasis on big books and on showing the pages of a book while reading aloud to children, I've found it a good technique to use non-illustrated books or to read a page before showing the pictures. This encourages children to listen and to show their listening skills when asked such questions as:

> *What was your favourite part of the story ?*
>
> *How do you think the animals felt when Tiddalik drank all the water?*

An important element in choosing stories to read aloud in this way is ensuring that they don't contain too many unfamiliar words or images. Of course the need to explain language will vary from school to school, depending on the experiences of the children. For example, children in the country may have had little experience of skyscrapers; many Aboriginal children will use *porcupine* for *echidna* when telling the story of 'The Echidna and the Shade Tree'. However, I don't mean that we should only use stories about known things — rather that we need to ensure our audience under-stand what a *squirrel, lorry* or *hedgehog* is like.

Getting children to retell a story either through drama, oral recall or sequencing of pictures is a much better way of encouraging oral language than asking questions like *What was the story about? Who was in the story?* Oral recall can be done well with the children sitting in a circle, each telling a little bit of the story and prompting others where necessary.

> A: In the Dreamtime there was a big frog
>
> B: called Tiddalik.
>
> C: He woke up one day and
>
> D: was very thirsty . . .

Other circle games and activities like 'I went shopping and I bought . . .' are great fun and reinforce turn-taking and listening skills. They should be played in a non-threatening manner, however: that is, no-one should be singled out or embarrassed if they can't remember. Such games give the teacher lots of opportunities to praise individual efforts and thus boost confidence. Children will often pick up on this praise and congratulate each other on good memories.

Daily news sessions perhaps cause teachers the most anguish when Aboriginal children are in the class, because they may be reluctant to participate, speak softly and look at the floor rather than at the audience. One way of overcoming such problems is to have a theme for news: for example, *This week we're going to tell everyone about what we do after school.* Even if some children still have little to say, gentle questioning (e.g. *Did you watch television or go to bed?*) will usually draw out some information.

After a child has given his or her news, the teacher may find it helpful to repeat it in a more structured way — like this:

> *Well, now we know that after school Tyrone played football in the backyard with his brother and then he had dinner. He watched 'Home and Away' before he went to bed. Thank you for telling us that, Tyrone.*

This young child has got stuck and is being helped out by a prompt chart. Such scaffolding builds confidence and helps all children.

This kind of paraphrase introduces children to the need for sequencing their ideas when they're telling a story. Some are confused by including details of lots of events (birthdays, Christmas, a new pet, dinner at McDonald's) all in one session, and so I try to limit news to describing one event.

Using a prompt chart (*Who? Where? When? Why? How did you feel? What happened next?*) is also helpful, not only for the child telling news but for the rest of the class, who are usually encouraged to ask questions about the news they've heard. If the teacher then retells the news, perhaps using a block for each part and building a tower, the class can tell which part wasn't mentioned and ask a question about it. I've found that children love these towers, competing with each other to build the tallest one and giving their approval to the children who do: *Wow, Tyrone used all the blocks today!*

My advice

All children enjoy play, want to be accepted by the group, want to achieve and appreciate praise that's deserved. Aboriginal children mix well within family and community and are quite self-assured and independent by the time they enter school. As teachers, we must do our best to provide an environment where we can recognise and build on these existing skills. Listen to what the children are saying and show them you value their contribution. The rewards are worth it.

Developing literacy skills through oral language activities

KATHLEEN RUSHTON

As we've already seen in Chapter 1, spoken and written language serve different purposes and hence have significantly different grammatical features. Aboriginal students begin school fluent in spoken English but, like other young learners, have had varying experiences of written language. Building on the oral language resources they bring to school contributes to their self-esteem and confidence and helps them to gain control over written forms of language.

The simple oral language games described below are designed for children in the early years of schooling who need support in using standard forms of English, or in using English for a range of different purposes.

Why the games were developed

The games originated in problems I perceived in some current early literacy practices. The common practice of using Show and Tell to develop students' oral language typically involves a *dialogue* between teacher and student: the student tells the class about something he or she has brought to school, while the teacher assists by asking questions, prompting or offering comments. The situation is highly contextualised: the student can point to whatever he or she is talking about. While children often enjoy this activity, I don't think that it helps to move them towards the many formal uses of oral language, or necessarily provides a springboard into writing. So, instead of Show and Tell, I use games for more focused language work in my classroom.

Another problem is connected with an equally common practice. In many early literacy programs, children are encouraged to 'write' (or have the teacher scribe) their own 'words' under a picture. While this helps to familiarise them with the processes of writing, it may well be that what's often viewed as 'poor' writing at a later stage is the result of recording oral language like this, without any systematic teaching of the structures of written language.

I believe that it's important to show children early on some of the ways in which information is organised differently in spoken and written texts. Even though they may not be able to read or write, they are quite capable of reproducing orally the structure of a written text and remembering its purpose and structure. So the purpose of the oral games presented here is to introduce some common written language structures in a simple, repetitive manner. The games scaffold early attempts at writing because students approach it with a better understanding of how language works.

The structure of the games ensures success for all students, and the teacher is always available as prompter and facilitator for those who need it. Each game introduces one of the following text types: description, instruction, narrative and recount. While aspects of all of these may be an incidental part of Show and Tell dialogue from time to time, in the games they are treated systematically and separately. Let's first look briefly at one of the games before considering how they might be organised into a program.

The description game

The following transcript comes from a Kindergarten classroom. Sam has a shoe box containing an object (a tube of glitter) that he will describe for the other students.

T: What are we going to play now? Put your hand up if you know the name.
S: Descriptions.
T: OK. Shake your box.
S: In my box is something which is . . . um . . . and it's got a lid on it and . . .
T: Something inside . . .
S: And there's something inside and it . . .
T: Sam, that's an excellent description.
L: You got a rock?
S: No.
T: Say it again, Sam.
S: In my box is something which is . . . it's plastic – see, it's not a rock – and it's got a lid on it and there's little squares with colours in it.

Instead of asking questions, the teacher is prompting. Sam knows that his tube of glitter is made of *plastic*, that it has a *lid* and that the shape of the pieces of glitter is *square*. However, to play the game he has to use a starter (*In my box is something which is . . .*) in order to construct a text with a structure (a beginning) and more formal language (*something which is . . .*).

The structure of the game generates the type of text required to give a description. Children are told in advance that size, shape, colour, characteristics and function are the features required in a description. Teacher interventions are explicit and are understood by the children because they're aware of the text structure. Thus they're able to take a major part in constructing a particular type of text from their own resources, and by the end of Kindergarten most require no prompting to produce one.

The description game is the first step towards producing an information report — on an animal, for example. Once students have mastered the game, they know what kind of information belongs to the description of an animal and don't offer personal anecdotes or preferences during joint construction of an information report. Other games introducing instructions, narratives and recounts can be played, and students learn what elements are necessary or optional in producing these types of writing. For example, they quickly appreciate that a personal comment is part of the structure of a recount but doesn't usually appear in an information report.

Incorporating the games into a classroom program

The games should be integrated with the rest of the term's work. Just as the description game is integrated with a focus on written information reports, the recount game will be integrated with a focus on reading and writing recounts. Fig. 7.2 shows how the games might be integrated with other key learning areas.

TERM	GAME FOCUS	INTEGRATION	READING & WRITING
1	Description	Science Maths	information reports descriptions of shape, length and mass
2	Instructions	Personal Development Visual Arts Maths	cooking – recipes craft – instructions instructions using positional vocabulary
3	Narrative	Personal Development Human Society	drama traditional oral and written narratives
4	Recount	Any area	excursions, events

FIG. 7.2. USING ORAL LANGUAGE GAMES ACROSS THE CURRICULUM

I use the games in place of regular news sessions. They take about half an hour a day if two or three students play each morning. Every session involves a weather activity and one of the games (usually one text type is focused on for several weeks at a time). The prompts are taught to the whole class, and then individual students volunteer or are selected to play the current game, with the class or myself providing prompts as necessary. However, my role during the games is to prompt for structure, not to correct oral language. Of course the games are also a means of developing students' vocabulary, since at this age they may not know the appropriate words to use in, say, a description. In such cases I provide the language to describe shape, colour, size or function and allow the student to repeat the whispered prompt to the class.

The games

Below are some further examples of games designed to teach the structures and some language features of a variety of text types.

Game 1: Instructions

An individual student chooses a procedure for which to give very basic instructions (e.g. how to read a book, make a cup of tea or drive a car). By adult standards, the instructions may well be simplified. The student provides the instructions one by one in response to whole class prompts (or chants) which have previously been taught and are prominently displayed in the classroom. Here's an example:

HOW TO PUT ON A JUMPER

Prompt (whole class)	Instructions – step by step (individual student)
1 First . . .	put your head through the big hole.
2 Then . . .	push your right arm in the sleeve.
3 Next . . .	put your other arm in the sleeve.
4 Finally . . .	pull the jumper down.

As part of teaching the language structure, the teacher needs to point out that the *process* (or verb) is placed first in the response, and that the class are providing the *linking* words.

Game 2: Narratives

One student makes up a narrative in response to whole class prompts (which are displayed in the classroom). The student answers one question at a time. Since coming up with an original story 'cold' can be quite difficult, it's likely that at first students will rely on retellings or variants of familiar stories, as in this example from late in the Kindergarten year:

Prompt (whole class)	Narrative (individual student)
1 When?	Once upon a time
2 Where?	in a dark forest
3 Who?	there was a beautiful princess.

4 What?	Her golden ball rolled into a stream.
5 Complication	An ugly toad said if she kissed him, he'd get her ball back for her.
6 Resolution/End	She did. He turned into a prince and they got married.

Game 3: Recounts

One student gives a recount in response to whole class prompts, answering one question at a time. Again the prompts are displayed.

Prompt	**Recount**
(whole class)	(individual student)
1 When?	Last Saturday
2 Where?	at home
3 Who?	my Grandma
4 What?	made me a whole chocolate cake.
5 Comment	It was yummy — I loved it.

The topics selected for the oral language games relate to children's immediate experiences and environment, but playing the games encourages them to speak in a way that resembles written English more closely than their everyday speech. The joint construction of written texts about specific topics is carefully prepared, and both then and during construction I make links with the games to draw on the knowledge of language structures and features that the children have built up.

Moving from spoken to written language

When students have had more experience of reading and writing, a similar approach can be taken at the conferencing and evaluation stages of writing. If students are taught the structures and grammatical features of particular text types, they have the resources to assess their own writing independently. The following example will demonstrate what I mean. It's drawn from a text written by Cynthia in Year 6. She had been asked to write a narrative, but instead she wrote a recount of a telemovie she had recently watched.

GETTING EVEN WITH DAD

One Saturday in Las Angelas Timmy had to stay at his dad's place and while he was there Timmy's dad stole of lot of precious coins which were worth about one hundred dollars. When they hid the coins Timmy was there watching them . . . Timmy's dad and his mates had to go out on a roller coaster and lots of other fun thing then one day Timmy hid them again and Timmy's dad got it and got in trouble by the police. But had proof he didn't do the robbery. Timmy decided to stay with his dad.

Even though Cynthia was aware of the narrative genre and its structure, she had produced an 'event-by-event' recount. It lacked many of the features we had been observing in effective models of narrative, such as the establishing of characters and settings and the movement from complication through successive tension-building events to a resolution and coda. As we had been working with functional grammar for some time, Cynthia was familiar with some of the different linguistic features which realise these aspects of text structure. So, as part of the conferencing, she was asked to list the processes she had used. This was the result:

relational	material	mental	verbal
(*being, having*)	(*doing*)	(*thinking, feeling*)	(*saying*)
was	had to stay	found out	tell
were	stole	decided	
was	hid		
had	went		
	got		
	hid		
	threatened		
	made		
	gave		
	had to go out		
	hid		
	got		
	got		

It was now clear to Cynthia that there was a predominance of material processes (event after event) and not a single mental process related to feelings. Realising that readers with scant information about the characters' motives or feelings were unlikely to engage with them or with the storyline, she now redrafted the text, including processes such as *felt* and *hope*. Here's an extract from her revised version:

> *. . . Timmy's father must have felt glad. Timmy decided to stay with his dad. Timmy and his father felt so happy that they celebrated. Timmy said 'Hope we will have a good time.' Timmy's father said 'Yeh let's go on the roller coaster again.'*

While there were still points to be explored with Cynthia, this second text was more engaging because readers could have some sympathy with the characters. Using her own resources, she had been able to develop her initial text and move from retelling to a written narrative. This ability to recognise and correct mistakes independently is crucial to students' self-esteem and motivation.

Conclusion

While the content of the curriculum needs special attention in the case of Aboriginal students, the development of literacy depends particularly on two points. Firstly, the role of the teacher is not to confront Aboriginal cultural values, but rather to facilitate literacy experiences that complement and build on the existing language experiences of the children. Secondly, the different uses of oral and written language must be recognised by students as well as teachers and considered in any classroom interaction. When this is done, students' oral language will be a resource for developing literacy.

Acknowledgement

We would like to acknowledge the role of the NSW Aboriginal Consultative Group Inc. in the preparation of this chapter, which has their endorsement.

8

Talking to persuade: debating in the classroom

VICKI POGULIS

Introduction

You've been told that you'll be taking debating for the year; you'll train teams and compete with other schools. You've had very little experience with debating, but your mind goes back to some horrific occasions at high school and you immediately turn red at the remembrance of your feeble attempts then!

That's exactly what happened to me, and so I started talking to people who knew more about it than I did. Some took it all so seriously, but it seemed to be a purely academic exercise in which teams tried to outsmart each other with clever words and arguments. I felt that there was more to it than that — indeed, I suspected that debating could turn out to be a very worthwhile means of stimulating students' thinking and improving their language skills.

What is debating and why teach it?

One of my favourite cartoons has a character saying, 'You do know what debate is, don't you?' — to which the other character responds, 'Of course I do! It's what you use to catch de fish!' Debating in your classroom may not catch many fish, but what you might catch is a method of teaching that brings together a number of curriculum areas in a very exciting way.

In everyday life we often argue, expressing opinions, taking a stand on something, or trying to convince someone to agree with us — all of which is perfectly natural human behaviour. Debating is simply an organised form of argument that involves looking at issues and justifying points of view. Formal debating has rules and conventions (discussed later in the chapter) which can easily be modified and used as a guide for less formal occasions in the classroom.

Debating teaches students how to construct and defend logical arguments, how to analyse arguments, and how to express themselves effectively to an audience. In other words, it helps them learn how to:

- think purposefully
- speak persuasively
- argue a point of view
- defend that view against an opposing one
- work cooperatively in a team.

One of the best ways to deal with problems is to encourage rational debate about them, for it is only by listening to other people's ideas and opinions that we learn to respect them. Debating can help us to isolate issues and see more clearly what a dispute is about. Equally, by expressing our own points of view, we can learn to plan and structure our thoughts in a more logical way.

Debating is a wonderful vehicle for teaching listening and speaking skills. Preparing for a debate gives students plenty of opportunities to speak informally as they discuss their approach; during the debate itself they will of course speak more formally. At all stages they will be listening, and they will listen with particular attention to the arguments advanced by their opponents.

Debating encourages students to look at the world around them. Many suitable topics straddle curriculum boundaries, and as long as they're selected with some care and imagination, students can engage in meaningful research, expanding their general knowledge and developing their comprehension skills. At the same time the particular purpose of their research encourages them to be critical of whatever they read or view as they work at clarifying their own ideas. It's a perfect illustration of what is sometimes called the Information Process (see Fig. 8.1). The written genres of argument and discussion (Derewianka 1990) belong here naturally too.

Defining	What do I really want to find out?
Locating	Where can I find the information I need?
Selecting	What information do I really need to use?
Organising	How can I best use this information?
Presenting	How can I present it?
Assessing	What did I learn from this?

(based on NSW Department of Education n.d.)

FIG. 8.1. THE INFORMATION PROCESS

Debating and cooperative learning

Apparently many teachers consider that the most important aspect of debating is the final presentation. However, I believe that all the activities involved in preparing a debating topic are of equal importance. And although formal debating is by its nature competitive, I see debating in the classroom as a cooperative rather than a competitive activity. It fosters attitudes of open-mindedness, fairness and tolerance of others. It provides for a range of abilities and temperaments and encourages students to learn the social skills needed to work in a team. All students in a class can take part in preparing for a debate (e.g. by gathering information, suggesting arguments, writing a speech, or listening to others speak). A student may be a researcher, speaker, chairperson, timekeeper, adjudicator, or whatever other role the teacher might like to nominate. Throughout the year, as different topics are debated, roles can be rotated; a class checklist will ensure that everyone's had a go at all of them.

Cooperative skills are an important aspect of debating in my classroom, and these in particular are explicitly taught and practised:

- forming groups
- communicating successfully within a group
- working in different group roles (e.g leader, scribe, reader, spokesperson)
- problem solving as a group
- managing differences.

Debating can be fun, it can be nerve-racking, and it's a great way to build classroom relationships. Indeed, handled sensitively by the teacher, it can develop many of the skills promoted by the Conflict Resolution Network, such as:

- a win/win approach (decisions that accommodate everyone's needs)
- creative responses (discerning opportunities the situation offers)
- empathy (the capacity to listen to others' viewpoints)
- appropriate assertiveness (being soft on the people, hard on the problem)
- cooperative power (working in a team)
- managing emotions (learning to articulate feelings clearly without putting people down)
- mapping the conflict (deciding on priorities)
- designing options (exploring possibilities)
- negotiation (settling the team's objectives)
- broadening perspectives (seeing the whole picture).

However, it's not only inside the classroom that debating builds relationships — it's also a great way for students and teachers to meet other classes and other schools. Everyone can learn more about approaching problems from a different standpoint and communicating effectively with people they don't know. A successful strategy I've used is to take experienced debaters from different schools and form mixed teams, give them a light-hearted topic (e.g. 'Ice cream should be banned') and after a short preparation time have them debate it. The students learn new ways of cooperating with each other and the teachers learn new ideas.

Strategies for teaching debating skills

It's crucial that team debating be preceded by modelling and various kinds of lead-up work. Lots of activities that involve talking and listening, arguing, persuading and working cooperatively provide suitable leads; here are some of them:

➤ Pair off students and ask them to present an agreed point of view on a variety of issues. Stress that opinions have to backed up with evidence.

➤ Take a newspaper article about a current topic, divide the class into two groups, for and against, and discuss the topic.

➤ Set up some brief role-plays (e.g. justify to your parent why you were late home from school — 'I helped a child who'd fallen over and hurt himself').

➤ Over a week, organise for each class member to prepare a short speech defending a particular position and present it to the class.

➤ Pair off students again and ask them all to pick a favourite book, film or TV show. They then take turns to explain their choice and justify it in face of their partner's questions.

➤ 'Just a Minute' is a game which begins with a student being selected to speak for one minute on a chosen topic. If there's a pause or repetition, or an irrelevant point is made, anyone in the class may challenge the speaker. A successful challenger has the next turn.

➤ Set up a role-play for the whole class or a large group within it. Begin with an issue (e.g. a road is to be built through bushland close to a suburban area) and allocate each student a pertinent role to play (e.g. surveyor, householder, schoolchild, labourer). Give them all cards outlining their role — for example:

> Householder. 35 years old. Is frightened
> for her two pre-schoolers when they play
> close to the bush.

Nominate two chairpersons and stage a discussion 'in the local hall' about whether the road should go ahead. Allow preparation time to suit the students' experience.

Introducing the notion of team debating

In formal debating there are two teams, each of three speakers, who are given a subject to debate. Preparation time may be limited but need not be. The team which supports the view expressed in the topic is called the *affirmative*, and the team which challenges that view is called the *negative*. Each team tries to persuade the audience to its own point of view. Speakers from the opposing teams speak alternately: the first speaker for the affirmative leads off, followed by the first speaker for the negative, the second speaker for the affirmative, and so on. In primary schools speeches generally last no more than three minutes.

- Welcome, ladies and gentlemen, to our debate. The topic for debate is:

  _____

- On my right is the affirmative team. The team consists of:
  _____ as first speaker
  _____ as second speaker
  _____ as third speaker.

- On my left is the negative team. The team consists of:
  _____ as first speaker
  _____ as second speaker
  _____ as third speaker.

- Speeches will be limited to three minutes each. The first bell will ring at the two-minute mark. The second bell will ring at the three-minute mark.

- I would now like to start the debate by calling upon the first speaker for the affirmative team.

- I now call upon the first speaker for the negative team.

- I now call upon the second speaker for the affirmative team.

- I now call upon the second speaker for the negative team.

- I now call upon the third and final speaker for the affirmative team.

- I will now call upon the final speaker for the negative team.

- That concludes our debate. We will wait for the adjudicator's decision.

- Thank you, ladies and gentlemen. We hope that you have enjoyed today's debate.

FIG 8.2. A SAMPLE CHAIRPERSON'S GUIDE SHEET

Against a backdrop of class texts about whales, these students are arguing in favour of a total ban on whale hunting. The girl in the middle is making notes to rebut some of the opposition's arguments.

On the occasion of a formal debate, there is a chairperson who welcomes the teams, introduces the topic, the speakers and the adjudicator, and offers congratulations and thanks as appropriate (for a sample chairperson's guide sheet, see Fig. 8.2). A timekeeper assists the chairperson, making sure that each team has exactly the same amount of time in which to argue its case.

An adjudicator or panel of adjudicators judges the debate and usually proffers advice and praise as well. Speakers and teams are judged in three areas:

matter: i.e. the content of the speech, and sometimes how it looks in written form — *the quality of what is said*

manner: i.e. the way a debater presents a speech, including style and intonation, persuasive ability and use of gesture — *presentation and the speaker's style*

method: i.e. the way a team organises and allocates ideas and points in their argument before and during the debate — *organisation and presentation of the best arguments in the time available*.

A sample adjudication sheet is reproduced as Fig. 8.3.

AFFIRMATIVE/NEGATIVE

	1st		2nd		3rd	
	Yes	No	Yes	No	Yes	No
Matter						
Were the arguments interesting and logical?						
Was there evidence of research, and was information accurate?						
Was the subject understood and explained clearly?						
Manner						
Was the speaker easy to hear?						
Did the speaker use his/her voice to advantage?						
Was the speaker's choice of language appropriate?						
Were the speaker's notes unobtrusive?						
Did the speaker's general appearance suggest confidence?						
Did the speaker seem to believe in what he/she was saying?						
Was the speaker persuasive?						
Method						
Was the speech well put together?						
Was the speaker's time used to good effect?						
Did the speaker give any indication of good team work?						
Did the speaker rebut the opposition's arguments effectively?						
TOTAL OF TICKS						

FIG. 8.3. SAMPLE ADJUDICATION SHEET FOR A FORMAL DEBATE

Adjudicators have two sheets, one for each team, and tick the appropriate columns.
The sheet can be simplified for informal debates.

Preparing a team debate

Basically debaters have to do two things:

- effectively present a team argument for or against a particular position
- listen to the other team's argument and then oppose it (a process known as *rebuttal*).

AFFIRMATIVE	NEGATIVE
First Speaker 1. Gives the topic. 2. Defines the topic and gives the case line (see main text). 3. Says what each speaker will do. 4. Introduces the main points of the team's argument.	**First Speaker** 1. Defines the topic and gives the case line. 2. Says what the team will do. 3. Introduces the main points of the team's argument. 4. Points out weaknesses in the affirmative's definition.
Second Speaker 1. Points out weaknesses of the first speaker for the negative. 2. Expounds the affirmative team's main arguments with supporting examples.	**Second Speaker** 1. Points out weaknesses of the second speaker for the affirmative. 2. Expounds the negative team's main arguments with supporting examples.
Third Speaker 1. Points out weaknesses of the negative team's position. 2. Sums up the affirmative team's argument.	**Third Speaker** 1. Points out weaknesses of the affirmative team's position. 2. Sums up the negative team's argument.

FIG. 8.4. THE TASKS OF THE SIX SPEAKERS IN A DEBATE

Each speaker in a team has a particular job, as set out in Fig. 8.4.

Preparing a debate is rather like looking at a tree. The roots of the tree are the *definition* (or *position*), the trunk is the *case line*, the branches are the *major points* of the argument and the leaves are the *examples*.

The team must first look at the topic very closely and decide what their definition is. Using a dictionary is helpful for defining key terms, but defining a topic word for word isn't necessarily very helpful. Let's take the topic 'Zoos are no place for animals' as an example. A satisfactory definition might be that zoos should be destroyed because they remove animals from their natural environment, confine them and continually expose them to close scrutiny.

Debating is not an individual exercise. Any team must work together, and a common line, a *case line*, should run through all their speeches. It could simply be an appropriate sentence repeated by each speaker, giving the audience and adjudicator a reference point throughout the debate — for example, 'We of the affirmative firmly believe that zoos are no place for animals because animals should be free to live in their natural environment'.

A team should prepare about six arguments in favour of their case, remembering that reference to published research, facts and figures strengthens any argument. Teams should also try to predict what arguments the other side might put forward and work out how to rebut them.

To leave a firm impression in the minds of the audience and adjudicator, speakers should always try to finish on a strong note. A pertinent quote, a rhetorical question or a repetition of the team's case line are good ways to end.

Steps in introducing team debating

I have found the following steps a valuable guide in teaching children about debating, both formal and informal.

Introducing the concept of a debate

1 Identify and discuss examples of team debates in the real world — parliamentary, humorous (e.g. World Series Debates), inter-school.

2 Try and arrange for the class to attend a debate — perhaps at a local high school, where you may be able to discuss with the teacher involved a particular focus you think your students need. The class could also attend meetings where informal debate takes place (e.g. a P & C or local council meeting).

3 As a class, try to come up with a definition of the term 'debate'. Begin with brainstorming and discuss suggestions until a satisfactory definition is agreed.

4 Introduce, teach and revise the basic rules and procedures. Summary charts and sheets are valuable as scaffolds in the early stages.

5 Similarly, introduce, teach and revise the roles of speakers.

Teaching how to prepare for a debate

1 Assess what your students need to prepare for a debate; you may find that along the way you have to demonstrate, provide models or teach particular skills (e.g. note-taking).

2 Choose a topic (see pp. 106–07 for some ideas).

3 Have the class (or team) define the key words of the topic.

4 Decide on the team's outline.

5 Brainstorm possible arguments.

6 Select the most appropriate ideas from the brainstorm.

7 Group the ideas into basic themes. Provide scaffolding in the form of worksheets to help students clarify their thoughts (see Fig. 8.5 for an example).

8 Think up examples for points in the argument.

A Great Debate

Topic: _____

Position: affirmative/negative

Three arguments to support my team:

1. _____
2. _____
3. _____

One of my points expanded:

_____

_____

Conclusion: _____

_____

FIG. 8.5. A STUDENT WORKSHEET

9 Allocate points and examples to individual speakers, who are then responsible (with teacher and class support) for preparing their own cases. You may need to help with researching arguments. Use electronic sources as well as paper-based materials. If your school is connected to the Internet, you have access to a huge source of (generally) up-to-date information; remember, however, that none of it has necessarily been vetted.

Tips for Speakers

- Practise speaking into a cassette recorder, play back the tape and note any words that are slurred, mumbled or mispronounced.
- Try to memorise only the main points when practising a speech. Speeches that are fully memorised tend to sound flat and lifeless.
- Speak, don't read (too much!) to the audience.
- Speak slowly. Use pauses and changes in volume for effect and emphasis.
- Use eye contact.
- Don't be afraid to include some humour.
- Use good, conversational English.
- Don't speak in a monotone — use all the variety in your voice.
- Stand confidently and try to control any nervous mannerisms.
- Gesture naturally — don't force it.
- Be yourself — convey your own personality. Relax!

FIG. 8.6. A STUDENT CHART

10 Discuss, model and analyse delivery (cf. the three critical aspects of debating — matter, manner and method — described on p. 95). Fig. 8.6 features a speaker's guide, which should be discussed, explicitly modelled and then distributed to students.

11 Provide lots of opportunities for students to practise delivery for themselves. Encourage them to present their speeches in a public setting, particularly to other classes in the school.

12 Finally, model, analyse and practise the skill of rebuttal, which involves listening and thinking 'on your feet'. It's discussed in the next section.

Teaching rebuttal

Because rebuttal can be a difficult concept to teach, I give students a card which helps them to remember the kinds of thing that make an opposing team's arguments vulnerable.

```
                    REASONS FOR REBUTTAL
    • There's a mistake in the argument (e.g. wrong statistic).
    • The argument has nothing to do with the topic.
    • The argument doesn't make sense.
    • The argument isn't important enough to mention.
    • The argument goes against the team's definition.
```

Here are a few useful activities for practising rebuttal:

➤ Whenever possible during the daily routine, ask students to give reasons for their answers in any subject area. You can extend their responses simply by asking *Why?*, *How?*, *Why do you think that?*, etc.

➤ Seat students in a circle with you and start by stating an opinion on a topic. The student on your left argues the weaknesses of your position and then states a further opinion on the topic. This continues around the circle.

➤ Tape segments of TV current affairs programs and ask students to jot down any points they consider weak in the arguments presented.

➤ Choose a topic and divide the class into affirmative and negative teams. Without preparation, the two teams take turns in advancing an argument supported by an example. If you deem an argument valid, a point is scored. Two points are scored if either team can refute an argument.

Providing feedback

As a rule I try not to score in debating. Enjoyment needs to be stressed in primary schools, and so I prefer to encourage all debaters by praising the good points and giving guidance for improvement. I also encourage students to provide each other with feedback. Reflection and self-evaluation are vital to improvement in any field of learning, and debating is no exception. Below are some ideas for involving your class in these processes:

- Use cassette players, cameras and video cameras to record your debaters at work.

- If a debate is formal and I want the class to be listening critically, I give each member of the audience an adjudication sheet (the specimen in Fig. 8.3 can be adapted to suit any particular class). After the debate, individuals' assessments are shared in a whole class discussion.

- Sometimes I get two students to share a sheet so that they have to negotiate their assessment.

- After both sides have stated their case in a debate, invite the audience to question the speakers or offer constructive criticism.

- To take a vote on the result of a debate, I have the class make coloured YES and NO signs and stick them on paddle-pop sticks. When the debate's over, they hold up one or other to register their verdict.

- To avoid making the voting process seem too serious or competitive, I sometimes devise methods that appeal to children's sense of humour. For example, I ask those who think that the affirmative side has 'won' to lie on their backs and wave their hands and feet in the air (the 'dead ant') and those who think the negative side has won to do star jumps. Something like this usually has everyone laughing!

Involving every member of the class in debating

It should already be clear that team debating can involve every member of the class. However, in this section I want to outline some further ways in which I make debating a part of classroom life.

Theme-linked debating topics

On the chalkboard I draw up a grid and, depending on the size of the class, write in four or five topics all based on the same theme, such as the Olympic Games (see Fig. 8.7). I like to have everyone in a team, though exceptions have to be made for the chairperson and the timekeeper. Usually I take the role of adjudicator. The students choose which topic they would like to

Affirmative Team	Topic	Negative Team
1. 2. 3.	The Olympics are about politics and economics, not sport.	1. 2. 3.
1. 2. 3.	Countries with a bad human rights record should not be allowed to compete in the Olympic Games.	1. 2. 3.
1. 2. 3.	The Olympic Games bring peace to the world.	1. 2. 3.
1. 2. 3.	Athletes should be allowed to use drugs to improve their performance.	1. 2. 3.
1. 2. 3.	The Olympic Games are about the best sporting countries in the world, not the best athletes.	1. 2. 3.

FIG. 8.7. A GRID FOR BOOKING TOPICS AND SPEAKING POSITIONS

debate and nominate on the grid which speaker they would like to be. They are allowed some time for preparation (normally two days), during which the chairperson and timekeeper act as 'roving researchers' and supporters. The debates are then presented to the class, other classes, invited parents, etc.

Back-up research support

If a class is working on a single debating topic requiring only six speakers, I form the rest of the class into back-up teams for each speaker, which means that everyone is involved in cooperative work. The teams can help with research and rehearsal for a speech (tape-recorders may be useful here too), conference written speeches through a 'writer's circle', and provide feedback after the debate.

Class projects linked to debate topics

I try to design projects that will reinforce the research skills students are using during preparation for a debate. For example, if the topic were 'Space travel is of no benefit to humankind', a complementary project might be to research the history of space travel in the twentieth century, make a model of a spacecraft and write an astronaut's diary.

Class excursions as a source of information

Excursions can sometimes be usefully associated with debating. For example, with a topic like 'Zoos should be banned', a zoo visit with its preparatory and follow-up work could focus on the issue of whether or not zoos perform a valuable role. 'Graffiti are art' is a topic which could provoke a walk around the local area, noting graffiti and contrasting them with officially sanctioned murals. Some classes might also make an excursion to a gallery of contemporary art.

Programming for and assessing debating

I try to make sure that any issue to be debated is relevant to the students and that I select a debating format suitable to their level of development. The following points are all considered when I am programming:

- student needs, skills and expertise
- the range of outcomes to be identified and addressed
- selection and design of activities to achieve the outcomes
- possibilities for integration across Key Learning Areas
- classroom management issues
- location of appropriate resources, including technology
- time allocation
- assessment and evaluation strategies.

I also make sure that I plan to cover:

- basic public speaking skills
- listening skills
- questioning strategies and techniques
- speaking with a purpose
- cooperative group work.

Throughout any debating work I use a checklist based on pointers from the NSW English K–6 syllabus (Fig. 8.8). It's invaluable for observing students' behaviour and monitoring achievement of the intended outcomes.

Topic:	Class:	Term:	Week/s:

STRAND	SUB-STRAND	POINTERS
TALKING AND LISTENING	Text and Context	Learning how to present a point of view on an issue and argue a case. Listening critically to debates, guided by a checklist.
	Strategies	Learning how to select, sequence and organise subject matter for prepared spoken presentations.
	Grammatical Patterns	Experimenting with ways of expressing modality.
READING	Text and Context	Learning how to use strategies such as skimming and scanning. Exploring symptoms of bias such as emotive language and exaggeration. Evaluating information from different sources.
	Learning to Read	Consolidating self-correcting reading strategies, such as re-reading, reading on and slowing down. Using appropriate pauses and emphasis when reading aloud. Attempting several strategies when reading difficult texts (e.g. making notes about key features).
	Grammar	Identifying text features which may help readers to distinguish fact from opinion.
WRITING	Text and Context	Writing discussions and expositions. Summarising and making notes.
	Learning to Write	Learning how to use drafting, revising, editing, proofreading and publishing. Developing a variety of spelling strategies. Writing speeches.
	Grammar	Selecting vocabulary for precise meaning.

FIG. 8.8. AN ASSESSMENT CHECKLIST

Debating topics readily become the theme for units of work. Then I find that making an overview is the most helpful first step in my programming. An example built around the topic 'Science is leading the world to destruction' is reproduced as Fig. 8.9.

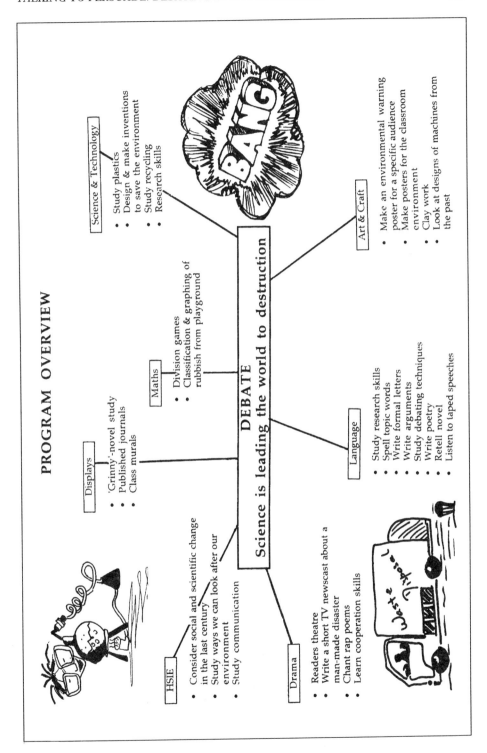

FIG. 8.9. OVERVIEW OF A UNIT BUILT AROUND A DEBATING TOPIC

KLA links

The choice of debating topic determines the links with different KLAs. Whenever I consult the syllabus for each KLA to see what's pertinent for my class, I also look for good, 'real' topics to debate. I find debating most effective when the topic focuses on community issues, so that students aren't debating just for the sake of it. Topics are sometimes chosen by the students, and it's great when parents become interested and suggest topics too.

While topics can emphasise a particular KLA, I've found that most topics reach across all of them. Here are some examples, beginning with a few centred on particular KLAs:

ENGLISH
Everyone in the world should learn English.
Books are a waste of time in our society.

MATHEMATICS
Lotteries should be banned.
There should be a unified system of measurement worldwide.

SCIENCE AND TECHNOLOGY
Computers should be used to replace teachers.
Inventors should be allowed to invent anything they like.

HSIE
Cars should be banned from the CBD.
School uniforms should be compulsory.

CREATIVE AND PRACTICAL ARTS
Songs with coarse language should be banned.
There should be no censorship.

PD/HEALTH/PE
There should be no Olympic Games.
Companies selling alcohol should not be allowed to advertise.

MORE GENERAL EXAMPLES
Australia should be a republic by the year 2000.
All Australian children should learn an Asian language.
Zoos shouldn't be allowed to exist anywhere in the world.
Police officers shouldn't carry guns.
Violence on the screen leads to violence on the streets.
Boys have it easier than girls.
Australia's political system is out of date.

Television is doing irreparable harm.
Camping is the ideal way of spending a holiday.
Capital punishment is the only way to deter criminals.
Discipline in schools should be firmer.
All luxury imports should be banned.
Australia should have a new flag.
Unemployed people should do community work.

The possibilities are endless, limited only by your imagination.

Conclusion

My hope is that debating in my classroom will be a living and exciting activity. I believe that through debating students learn skills they can take with them and use all their lives — improved language skills, the ability to see that there's always more than one viewpoint on an issue, and the capacity to live tolerantly alongside others in our society.

9

Voice matters

ISOBEL KIRK

The way you talk is more important than the way you look. It is how you communicate with the outside world that determines your position within it. Even though we like to think we live in a democratic society, people judge us by the way we speak.

(Lillian Glass)

Every week I teach voice and communication skills to some of Australia's leading corporate executives and decision makers. They have come through an education system which produces technocrats — experts in medicine, law, science, engineering, accounting — yet they're unable to communicate effectively. Many times I've witnessed the result of months of board room preparation, power dressing and perfect speech content go down the gurgler when they open their mouths.

People make astonishing judgements about us based on the way we speak — about our intelligence, education, income and sex appeal. How many silent movie stars found themselves on the scrap heap overnight because of the sound of their voices? *Voices arouse such an immediate emotional response that if you can make yours work for you, you have a very powerful tool at your command.*

Why do we have a voice?

Basically our voices are part of our survival armoury: like other animals we use them to ward off predators and attract mates. However, human voices are deliciously subtle; they seem designed to reveal our feelings. Listen to us at a sporting event (it's as if someone in the sky lowers down a placard saying,

'This is your vowel and this is your pitch', as we *ooohhh* and *awwwww* and *yeeeeaaahhhh*); hear us during grieving, during sex, during childbirth, or when we communicate with a pre-language baby or toddler. Our meaning is clear and transfers instantly from human to human — we don't need to consult a book to decide what is meant by that particular sigh, squeal or wail. This is the raw sound, by turns powerful and delicate, that conveys our feelings — vibrations carrying outwards signals from our inner emotional world. This is the stream of sound that we divide and shape with lips and tongue to form words, to express our thoughts.

What is the goal in communication?

Briefly, it is to *think, feel, speak and breathe simultaneously.* Everyone has a voice capable of expressing all their feelings, using a three-to-four octave range. We are born able to make all the sounds in every language in the world: Kalahari bushman clicks, Dutch throaty 'g's, French 'r's, English 'th's. But by nine months of age we begin to limit ourselves to the sounds we hear around us, and the life-long business of muzzling our voices has begun.

Why muzzle the voice?

Our society doesn't encourage the revelation of feelings. Early on we get messages not to be so noisy or not to be so rude. We begin to constrict our voices to protect ourselves. The most efficient way to do this is to impede our breath and constrict the bellows which powers these embarrassing sounds. We hold in at many different points, and for each person the combination of muscle tensions is different, just as fingerprints are. Here are some of the most common self-protective devices:

> toes curl; knees lock; thighs are squeezed; buttocks tighten; hip sockets become rigid; stomach muscles pull in (stopping the diaphragm from flattening); ribs are held tight; shoulder blades stiffen; breastbone is grabbed by surrounding muscle (shutting down the solar plexus); upper chest freezes; neck tightens; jaw locks; tongue bunches; soft palate droops; eyes deaden; forehead clenches; scalp contracts.

These are all brilliant devices to suppress emotion and prevent it from leaking or bursting out. Unfortunately quite young children learn to clamp down their bodies; they are left grabbing little thimblefuls of air from under their collar-bones, and they have thin little voices.

The first step is to methodically undo restrictive muscle tensions and emotional/ psychological inhibitions. When this basic work is done, the improvement inevitably flows through to presentation and public speaking.

The good news

If people are encouraged to let their voices out to play, to enjoy the rich sounds we human animals can produce, they very rapidly rediscover the joys of uninhibited release and self-expression they knew as babies.

Yes, I know, students 'express themselves' in the playground with no hesitation at all — the trouble is that the free sounds they produce there are choked by formal or challenging situations like presenting, debating or performing. How often have I spent the whole of a session giving exercises to free up the voice (to which my earnest students respond with feeble peeps), only to hear at the end of class, bellowed across the room, 'Hey, you going down the pub later?', with answering shrieks and outpourings of vitality and energy.

Everyone sounds great rehearsing at home or singing in the bath. It's only when faced with a (sometimes unconsciously) perceived threat that we humans shut down, and unfortunately public speaking is widely perceived as threatening. Indeed, surveys in the US show that most people fear public speaking more than death! Clearly the earlier we encourage students to take off their gags and let themselves speak, the more comfortable they will feel as public speakers. *In this country you have only to be a very good speaker to be head and shoulders above the rest.*

Things to do

Some years ago I was asked to talk about voice to my son's Year 5 class. It seemed a good idea to give them the same lesson as I give students on their first day at NIDA, where I begin by asking, 'What is your voice?'

After some chat the answer comes, 'Vibration'.

'What is vibration?'

A bit more chat; we talk about how vibration is like electricity, physical but invisible.

'How can we feel vibrations?'

Everyone blows up a balloon and hums and haas into it, feeling it vibrate; they hold one between two mouths and hum — any imaginative thing they can do to feel vibrations, first through the hands and then moving the balloon all over the body. Perfectly sensible people go silly with balloons, and so sometimes I put on the music 'Good Vibrations' and let them play, culminating with a big bursting vibration to get rid of the wretched things.

Then they hum, feeling their throat, cheeks and chest for vibrations, noticing where these are strongest and encouraging the gentle ones (e.g. on the top of the head).

Next they form pairs and A hums on any note, with a new note for each breath, while B feels A's head, nose, back, etc. With some groups I encourage

Exploring your voice can always be fun, as it obviously was for these boys while they felt for the vibrations of humming.

B to feel all over the humming body — legs, toes, arms, etc. — to see how many places vibrations might go to. At the same time I ask A to imagine sending vibrations to weird and wonderful places, to make them flow freely and sensuously through all the bones in the body. This exercise does not work with barristers, civil engineers or bankers!

Why focus on encouraging vibrations? Because the more there are, the stronger the sound, proving that volume or projection is the result of relaxation and a free breath rather than effortfully pushing the voice. *Trying harder is the worst instruction we can give to any voice.* It just crawls tighter into its protective little ball.

And what carries the vibrations from inside outwards? The short answer is air, or breath. I have a pop-up book showing the skeleton, lungs, diaphragm and so on, and whenever possible I get hold of a skeleton, full-size or a plastic toy, to show in rudimentary fashion how the breath works (cf. Fig. 9.1). We talk about a bellows and how air must support the vibrations. The deeper the source of the breath, the better supported the sound.

Breath awareness

1 Beginning with both hands placed on the soft little triangle of the solar plexus, where the ribs meet the breastbone, dig in and around the rib cage to see how sturdy the bones are and how far they go down at the waist. Notice the room between the bottom of the rib cage and the hips, and give a little hula wiggle to encourage mobility.

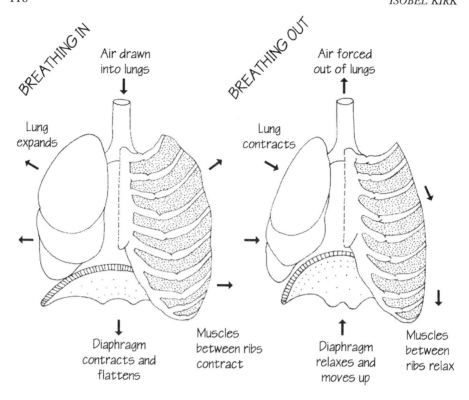

FIG 9.1. MECHANISMS OF RESPIRATION

2   Either in pairs or alone, it's agreeable to explore all the different places breath can move to, and to remind muscles to let go and release. Cutting off the lower places for breath has a dramatic effect on the power of the voice. *The deeper the relaxation, the deeper the breath and the richer and fuller the voice.*

3   Put one hand on each side where the ribs bulge and feel the breath expanding the rib cage, moving your hands apart.

4   Place your hands to overlap on the breastbone and feel the upper chest expand, moving your nipples apart.

5   Feel the lower back moving in and out with breath. It's useful to bend over as if you were hanging by your tailbone, with knees slightly bent and hands on the lower back — this position encourages breath to move around the tailbone.

6   Sit in a squat and feel the breath down in the tailbone and belly. Squatting is a good position for voice exercises as it makes it almost impossible for the breath to centre in the upper chest. If the upper arms are inside the

thighs during the squat and slightly pushing the knees apart, the hip bones loosen and become more flexible, allowing the experience of breath to be very deep.

7 Here's a rather cheeky exercise everyone loves, showing how the muscles of the lower torso are involved with breath. First, feed in a little cough. Do it again and notice what happens to the sphincter muscles. If there's a response down there, it's a good indication that the bottom half of the body is reasonably relaxed and the breath is dropping nice and deeply. (My barrister classes are quite idiotic about this exercise and have incorporated the anus cough before many presentations as an in-joke.)

Adding vibration to the breath

Combine the breath with vibration by sighing a few times on different notes and playing about with different vowels and vowel combinations. Students sometimes like to have a conversation with just these open sounds and no language at all.

Chopping up the sound into language

This is an adaptation of an exercise from my dear friend and teacher, Kristin Linklater.

1 Everyone finds a space on the floor with lots of room to explore as many different ways as possible to stop and start sound. Any open sound will do; it's fun to encourage weird and wonderful noises. Roll across the floor and bounce sound out of your bottom; stop it with your knee, then release it; thump your chest; raspberry on your arm to half-stop it — the possibilities are endless. Let this be as physical and crazy as possible (I encourage students to pinch each other's ideas if they like the look of them).

2 Eventually everyone demonstrates their favourite sound and action.

3 Given a bit of time, students choose three very different ways to stop and start sound. They rehearse these so that they can flow quickly from one to the next.

4 Everyone performs their 'word' for the others. This can be taken further by pairing students and encouraging them to have a conversation with their partner using their newly evolved primitive language.

5 Inching towards speech, ask the students to stop and start sounds again, now using just their lips and tongue. This can lead to gibberish games, exploring sounds in other languages, modern sound poetry or even Middle English! Most particularly, it's a great preparation for work on consonants.

Consonants

Ninety per cent of Australians' voices (including those whose mother tongue is not English) can be improved dramatically by using more energy on consonants. Practise speech on a whisper, discovering and accentuating the consonants. Then say the same words aloud, recapturing the same energy.

Vocal colour and emphasis

People often complain to me that their voices are dull and monotonous. They worry because they sound uninterested in their subject, when within themselves they are enthusiastic and excited. They feel frustrated because audiences quickly lose interest and ignore or overlook their contributions. 'Help me give my voice more colour!' they beg.

Most languages indicate the important words in the sentence by means of word order, grammatical endings, systems of tones and pitch, etc. With English, we often keep the same sentence structure and indicate the important words by stress. I once worked with a Polish actor who had the lead in an internationally funded Australian movie. The director rang and said, 'His English is perfect, crystal clear. I just can't understand a single word he says!' So I asked the actor to say in Polish:

She saw me?

She *saw* me?

She saw *me*?

In his mother tongue the grammar changed each time but the stresses stayed the same. Once he learnt how we vary our emphasis and play with colour, he was able to express different attitudes and emotions and inject subtle nuances.

We emphasise and colour our language by changing pitch, using combinations of ever-changing notes, lengthening and shortening vowels to change the rhythm, twisting, flicking, dabbing and wringing our words, and just generally messing about in a thousand different ways. We have voices capable of a large pitch range — say, 3–4 octaves (though work being done in France indicates 10 octaves!). So we have lots of notes, and on just one note we can change through countless different sounds. Most animals have a fairly limited choice.

Exercises for variety and emphasis: developing flexibility and agility of the voice

Here are some exercises I remember from my student days at NIDA thirty years ago; with some adaptations, I still enjoy using them today.

Pitch

1 Count from one to ten, taking a breath before each numeral and prolonging the vowel in each word to three or four times its normal length. Ask the students to repeat each word after you.

   a) Give each numeral a quiet, prolonged upward inflection, as if asking a question.

   b) Use a stronger upward inflection, expressing surprise.

   c) Use a prolonged downward inflection, suggesting a quiet finality.

   d) Increase the strength and abruptness of the downward inflection to suggest a more positive conviction.

   e) Everyone has a turn, exaggerating and playing with inflections (and maybe guessing the various meanings).

   f) Whine with a little puppy sound, very softly, from the top of your voice to the very bottom. See how high and low you can go.

   g) Put your finger on your voice box (or someone else's) to feel it moving up at the top of the whine and down at the bottom.

2 After isolating pitch change as a form of emphasis, you can move on to explore how we show which is the important word in the sentence.

   Count from one to five as if asking a question, going up in pitch on each word and emphasising one of the numerals. For example, A asks B, '*One*, two, three, four, five?' and B answers (starting high and going low), '*One*, two, three, four, five'. B asks C (starting low and going high), 'One, *two*, three, four, five?' and C answers, 'One, *two*, three, four, five'. And so on — it's fun to exaggerate all the changes.

   Often we get louder on an important word, but there are more interesting ways to achieve emphasis. For example, the vowel in the important word can be stretched and the vowels in the words on either side shortened, which gives the sentence rhythm. There's a shorter, lighter beat or syncopation immediately before the important word and a slightly longer one immediately after. This becomes obvious in rapping, and I've found that kids immediately understand the jokes implied when the rap rhythm changes. It's a good idea to play some rap and learn one of the songs (adults find it quite challenging, but primary children have no trouble at all). Sometimes my NIDA students perform a poem we're studying as a rap number.

Inching towards language

1 Say 'Oh', suggesting the meanings listed below. Make the meaning very clear through exaggeration — 'ugly' sounds are absolutely fine. What sort of emphases are used? Pitch, rhythm, vowel changes?

  a) mild surprise

  b) great surprise

  c) polite interest

  d) marked indifference

  e) disappointment

  f) pity (the poor thing!)

  g) disgust

  h) sarcasm (I told you so!)

  i) pleased surprise

2 Say 'She saw me', suggesting the following different meanings:

  a) asking a question (emphasise alternatively she, saw and me)

  b) pleased surprise

  c) horrified surprise

  d) stout affirmation (she did, too!)

  e) sarcasm (she wouldn't look at me!)

3 Ask 'Why did you do that?' as a mere request for information, and successively to express surprise, accusation, anger and despair.

4 Portray the following meanings:

  a) 'Oh, he did?' (surprise)

  b) 'Oh, he did!' (a threat; I'll see about that!)

  c) 'Oh, he did!' (fear)

  d) 'Oh, he did!' (jeering)

  e) 'You won't mind, will you?' (fearful that you will)

  f) 'You won't mind, will you?' (of course you won't)

  g) 'You are going, aren't you?' (I want to know)

  h) 'You are going, aren't you?' (of course you're going)

  i) 'He was pretty good' (he was really very good)

  j) 'He was pretty good' (he was only fair)

5 Read the sentence 'We are all going' to suggest such meanings as surprise, defiance, disappointment, disgust and sarcasm. In how many different ways can this short sentence be spoken?

6 How many different meanings can you read into the expression 'You were wonderful'? A few are suggested below:

  a) warmly (from an enthusiastic admirer)

b) statement (you were good; the others were bad)

c) statement (you used to be good but you aren't any more)

d) with surprise (I expected you'd be pretty bad)

e) as a question (I'm glad to hear that you were a success)

f) politely (you were really pretty bad)

g) sarcastically

In how many different ways can this be said so that the real meaning runs counter to the surface meaning?

7 Say 'Hello' in a number of different ways: as a greeting to an old friend, as an exclamation of surprise, as a teacher greeting one of her pupils, as a crusty old boss to his employee, and as a call to attract attention.

8 Once a complete dramatic sketch was written in which the chief character spoke just two words, 'Come here', varying the expression for each change of situation. Speak the same two words to suit the various situations sketched below:

a) Your small sister is teasing the cat. You call her to tell her to stop it.

b) Now it's your friend's sister, whom you don't particularly like.

c) Your pet rat is about to run up the teacher's leg. You pretend to call it.

d) You call your dog in a friendly fashion.

e) You see across the playground a friend you haven't seen for ages. You call to attract his attention.

f) You're swimming out beyond your depth; suddenly you become frightened and call out.

g) You excitedly read in the paper that you've won an important contest. You want to show your friend.

h) You're walking along the beach when you suddenly discover something very interesting and curious; you've never seen anything like it before. You call your friend.

i) You're a teacher. The school bully has gone one step too far; you determine to have it out with him (or her). Very sternly you tell him to come to the front of the room.

j) You're suddenly woken by a noise coming from outside. Cautiously you creep to the window and look out. In the dim light you see in the yard below a dark figure attempting to force a window. Frightened, you call in a 'stage whisper' to your roommate.

In all the exercises outlined above, the importance lies not just in expressing the varying meanings, but also in noticing the different ways we emphasise and colour the words.

Moving into a public forum

All the voice and text work done in class is primarily to loosen the voice and introduce students to the fun to be had in playing with sounds, which can then be translated into enjoyment of language and the rich and melodic sounds contained within language. When I'm presented with an actor who mumbles, this is the path I always take — first let the voice out of its social straitjacket and then play with poetry or some rich text (Shakespeare is excellent as long as it's handled irreverently). This encourages the student to ingest the words, chew them and spit them out with relish.

There does come a time, however, when students have to move into a public forum and make a presentation to a larger audience. Usually all they need to be reminded of is a few key points. Too many instructions can overload a performer, and hey presto! the voice becomes muzzled again. Below are a few points which are often helpful to students involved in debating or public speaking.

Three do's and don'ts

1 Do speak with passion and interest. If you don't care, we won't care.
2 Do breathe! Not by sucking in gusts of air, but by allowing air to be brought into the body by the thought. Every new thought brings in a new breath.
3 Do kiss the 'voice beautiful' goodbye. Try all types of sounds to express yourself.

1 Don't read a speech. Adlib to points on the page and keep eye contact with your audience.
2 Don't try to say too much. We're more interested in you than in facts.
3 Don't tell jokes. Even professional comics have trouble with them.

When directing

Taking part in a play puts more exacting demands on students' voices. If you're directing, do remember to differentiate between *hear* and *understand*. Sometimes we tell performers, 'I can't hear you'. So they speak louder and louder, pushing their voices, thrusting necks forward and tightening throats. This only exacerbates the problem, making any audience recoil in their seats — it's rather like being cornered by a jackhammer. What we really mean is we can't understand them. In such cases, ask them to use more energy on the consonants.

A quickie voice and body warm-up to do every day

This is particularly helpful before any formal presentation, and it's good for your voice too!

- Feet rather far apart, lean to each side to stretch the *side* ribs.
- Banana stretch (arms up over the head, stretch evenly backwards) for the *front* ribs.
- Hug a tree, arms curved in front, rounding the spine for the *back* ribs.
- Yawn and stretch luxuriously through the whole body, allowing all manner of weird and wonderful sounds to squeak, grunt and pour out of you.
- *Stretch* the arms right up to the sky, keep them tight, then let your fingers . . . wrists . . . elbows drop in sequence towards the floor, letting them give in to the pull of gravity.
- *Sigh a deep breath* into the lower back ribs.
- Roll the head gently and carefully to loosen the *neck*.
- Stretch the *lips* by inserting two fingers at each side of the mouth.
- Hum, feeling the vibrations on the lips and inside the mouth on the hard palate, behind the top front teeth. Any humming exercise that is free and relaxed is excellent.
- Bounce your *shoulder blades* loosely, letting sounds bounce out of you any which way.
- Bounce your *knees* loosely, letting sounds fly out.
- Bounce on the balls of your *feet* as if you have springs underneath them, again allowing any loose free sounds to escape.
- Sigh four deep-down sighs, imagining breath can move around in the *bottom* of your body.
- Sigh six sighs with your hands on your sides, feeling air moving into the *side ribs*.
- Pant like a puppy for about ten seconds, then sigh with relief. Rest and pant again at any speed that feels interesting to you, then vary the speed from slow to fast. Repeat this pattern four or five times.
- Repeat the above, this time using your voice and letting sounds come easily and freely from you. Suspend any aesthetic judgement and allow your voice to touch any note it likes, high or low or in the middle. You may wish to explore a pitch you feel quite comfortable with and then move to one you usually avoid.
- Basically you are letting your voice out to play, with all the colour and energy and variation you can find.

TRY OUT YOUR VOICE ON SOMETHING
SATISFYING AND WONDERFUL!

10

Talk about literacy in the content areas

PAULINE JONES

As we've seen in Chapter 1, pre-school language experience mainly involves children in learning spoken language so as to have their basic needs met, get along with others, and explore the world. In this way they build up a considerable knowledge of language, though as yet they are scarcely conscious of it. School, however, will bring them some awareness of language as a complex system of sounds and symbols for expressing ideas and communicating information in an infinite variety of situations.

The primary years are of course crucial for extending the child's repertoire of spoken language skills. Yet they are equally crucial for developing literacy skills across the curriculum, and so this chapter focuses on ways in which talk can be built into a model for teaching literacy — where it has a pivotal role to play.

Talk about literacy can be seen as three-dimensional: talk about the topic or content, talk as a bridge to writing, and talk about texts. Effective literacy programs address all three aspects, and they are discussed separately below.

Talk about content or topic

A lot of talk will be about the topics (or fields) associated with the primary school curriculum; indeed, curriculum content may be seen as constructed through talk. Concepts and ideas become known or understood through interactions between children and teachers and texts (and other artefacts). Children encounter new ways of considering everyday phenomena. For example, *rain*, *fog* and *dew* become known in the subject area of Science as elements in the Water Cycle, and children learn to regard their common-sense knowledge of weather in a more abstract way in order to articulate the processes of evaporation and precipitation. Such abstract or 'uncommonsense' concepts are typically expressed in technical language. However, the conceptual leap required to go from observed everyday experience to technical (often written) language is considerable, and children generally rely on spoken language to help them make it (Egan 1991; Unsworth 1993). Thus talk can be seen as a tool for thinking and communicating in subject-specific ways.

Talk as a bridge to writing

Topics are very often introduced and built up through experiences in which talk accompanies some type of activity — hence the term 'language accompanying action'. If you turn back to Fig. 2.1 (p. 13), you'll see that this kind of language stands at one end of the mode continuum. One way of describing language and literacy learning in the primary years is as a gradual shift along the continuum towards the more abstract, written-like language that characterises the subject areas of secondary school. But students need support to move into these more literate ways of 'knowing', and talk is perhaps the most important component in that support. As Gibbons (1993) observes, talk can be said to provide a bridge, or staging point, in a student's progress from oral to written language.

Talk about texts

Associated with new ways of using language are new understandings generated by critical reflection about language and text. At school, texts become objects of study as well as sources of pleasure and information. For example, children begin to consider the power of language to:

- present knowledge in particular ways (e.g. in subject-specific ways)
- construct realities (e.g. fantasy and historical texts)
- produce versions of reality (e.g. everyday life as presented in junk mail catalogues or soap operas)
- position individuals according to factors like gender, class or age (e.g. the representations of women and men in fairytales)
- persuade people to particular actions (e.g. letters of complaint, election advertisements).

It's possible to consider such factors largely because there's an unavoidable relationship between text and context. Ideologies and influences like those mentioned above, all of which arise from the context of culture, find expression in texts through the language choices made by speakers or writers.

Spoken language has a key role to play in the development of critical literacy skills. It's not enough for teachers to provide a range of texts (literary, factual, media and everyday) and ask students to 'interrogate' them; they have to be shown how to take them apart. They need tools for identifying and discussing language choices, for deconstructing values and ideas (both explicit and implicit), and for debating possible readings. They need the right kinds of terms (which they will use more often in speech than in writing). In other words, they have to develop a metalanguage — a set of shared understandings about language and texts built up over time. In many classrooms technical talk of this kind is commonplace: students learn to use increasingly sophisticated terms, some related to discourses (e.g. Science and Technology), some to the context of culture (e.g. to identify sexism or racism), some to the generic staging of text types (e.g. the structure of narratives), and some to language features or grammar (e.g. participants, processes).

A role for the teacher

A literacy program which incorporates these three aspects of talk demands particular things of teachers. In a sense their role, though more consciously planned and less intimate, mirrors that of parents or caregivers in a young child's learning of his or her mother tongue. Like parents, they are concerned with helping learners to make sense of their worlds and develop language skills across a range of contexts. To this end, they plan the types of activities which foster interchange about class topics between themselves and their students, and between individual students. Nevertheless there are moments when they need to explicitly teach understandings in the content area or about language itself, just as a parent or caregiver points out aspects of language use to a young child.

Painter (1986) found that young children jointly construct text in interactions with adult caregivers. As they talk about shared experiences, adults respond to children's utterances, extend them and sometimes make salient points about language. These repeated interactions enable children to internalise the models of language they've heard and eventually to use them to construct new texts. Similarly, as children encounter new subjects and topics at school, teachers need to provide considerable support and guidance, their role varying from that of facilitator or guide to that of a more interventionist 'expert' who makes explicit the ways in which particular meanings are achieved.

Often children need support at the beginning of a task. Here student and teacher share their first language, Greek, as they locate and select art materials.

A further responsibility for teachers is the staging or sequencing of experiences so that, over time, children are able to move to independent use of spoken and written language across a range of content areas. Teachers need to plan units of work which take children from what they know to what they don't — which stretch their understandings of language in general, as well as the language belonging to particular curriculum areas. Consequently teachers have to research content areas and become familiar with the language skills of their students and the demands of the curriculum.

A teaching-learning cycle

In planning a unit of work, teachers need a framework for staging teaching and learning that integrates talking and listening with reading and writing, accommodates literacy talk in all its dimensions and allows for a flexible teacher role. Many teachers draw on a curriculum cycle developed as part of the Disadvantaged Schools Program in Sydney, which is summarised in Fig. 10.1. It's an effective model for teaching speaking and listening skills within the context of literacy across the curriculum.

The cycle consists of four stages: Negotiating Field, Deconstruction, Joint Construction and Independent Construction. It's not a lock-step model — indeed teachers use the cycle in many different ways — but it does assume that learners move from the teacher-supported initial stages through joint construction to independent construction. This progression parallels the general model of interaction in language development observed by Painter. Let's now look at the stages of the cycle in a little more detail and try to identify the points at which opportunities for talk arise.

Negotiating the field

In this initial stage, when teachers and students open up the field or topic to be investigated, define it and decide which aspects will be relevant, talk as process will be very evident. Through talk, teachers can find out what their students already know and whether they possess any particular strengths, while students will get an idea of the purpose and scope of their study. At this point many teachers encourage students to nominate the direction that investigations might take and suggest the types of activity that might be undertaken.

For example, in a unit of work on Australian animals, older primary children might brainstorm what they already know and identify some of the things they'd like to find out or issues they want to pursue. If they're familiar with a number of different text types, they could then list possibilities with a view to selecting one to focus on (e.g. information reports about particular animals, discussions about kangaroo culling, or instructions for caring for injured animals).

Teachers of younger children frequently begin with structured play (e.g. free construction with scrap materials), direct observation (e.g. caterpillars or snails in a large transparent container), or guided experience (e.g. making toast). The activity itself usually provides an excellent opportunity for children to 'talk (and listen) while they do', and to begin using vocabulary specific to the topic. This 'language accompanying action' helps them build first-hand knowledge of the field. However, as we saw with the lettuce-planting example in Chapter 2, these types of activity at the *action* end of the mode continuum don't necessarily give students access to the more specific language and understandings associated with a particular field; they may simply provide an entry point, assuming other activities that will move children towards understandings at the *reflection* end of the continuum.

On completion of the activity, teacher and children can discuss ways to record the experience for varying purposes and audiences. For example, they

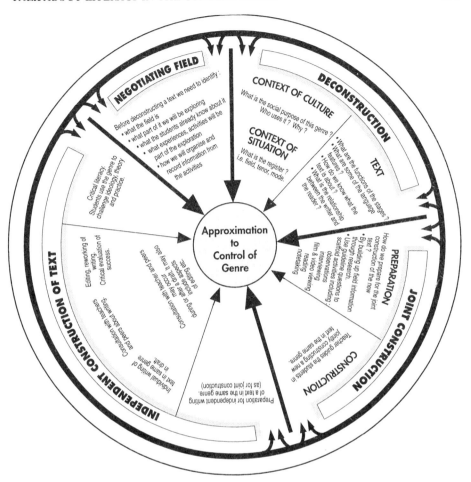

FIG. 10.1. A CURRICULUM CYCLE (from Met. East DSP 1992)

might decide that a labelled diagram would be enough to help them remember what they made from scrap material, but telling someone else how to copy the model would require some instructions. However, once a clear purpose for the subsequent learning activities has been established (e.g. *because we want to cut down on the amount of garbage we throw out, we're going to look at some fun ways to reuse materials*), it's possible to define purposes for reading and writing and an associated text type. Of course, the degree of negotiation possible varies from class to class, and in many cases decisions about topic or text type may be made outside the classroom.

This introductory stage is crucial because it influences the type of motivation and engagement learners will have with the topic. There are a number of ways in which teachers introduce topics, but some kind of discussion is commonplace. Whether it takes place amongst the whole class, or in small groups or pairs, it's important for students to be able to pool and clarify information and make decisions about their future direction. Class discussions are most effective when there's some visual support in the shape of posters, big books, demonstrations or models. One teacher began a unit of work on Levers and Pulleys by taking apart a sash window similar to those built into the classroom, thus enabling all her students to make a connection between the curriculum topic and their lived experience.

Once topic and text type have been negotiated, teachers and students usually move on to either the Deconstruction or Joint Construction stages.

Deconstruction

At this stage, teachers and students examine the context in which a text is produced as well as the text itself. For example, a class studying procedures might ask the following questions about a recipe given away in butchers' shops:

What is the purpose of this text? (*to encourage shoppers to buy particular types of meat; to choose meat with little fat*)

Who wrote it? (*a person or team of people employed by the meat industry*)

Who is meant to read it? (*busy people; cooks looking for new ideas*)

How does it work? (*small glossy cards arranged at eye height; simple layout with photograph; food looks good, as if a chef has produced it; ingredients usually easy to get if you live near the shops; recipes aren't too hard*)

The context of situation is also considered:

What is the text about? (*food, meat, cooking*)

What relationships exist between reader and writer? (*expert to learner who is not an absolute beginner but may need more information about health*)

What part does language play in the activity? (*written text carries most of the detail, though some information is in photos or the reader's head*)

Initially deconstruction requires teachers to take an active role in pointing out some of the conventions of language use. However, once students are familiar with a number of basic terms, the teacher can take a less prominent role. For example, students might be split into small groups and given an assortment of texts (including student-written and real life factual texts, advertising literature and posters) and asked to consider them using the criteria set out above. (A worksheet listing the questions is a useful adjunct here.) Discussion at this stage will mostly be talk as process, but if students are asked to share their group's findings with the rest of the class, they will have to use more performance-orientated language.

As well as deconstructing context, students and teachers deconstruct text. Generally the focus is on the structure or stages of the text (e.g. *What information is there in this part?*) and some associated language features (e.g. *What else do you notice about this particular type of text? Are there any special words?*). Naturally teachers need to provide key terms while their students are gaining control over the metalanguage. However, most adapt quite easily to using technical terms at the levels of text (e.g. *procedure, recount*), structure (e.g. *orientation, sequence of events, reorientation*) and grammar (e.g. *circumstances, connectives*). Such terms give them the means of expressing increasingly sophisticated understandings about language.

There are a number of activities teachers commonly use to develop understandings about text. They include cloze activities which focus on particular language features, text sorting (mentioned above), jumbled texts which highlight text structure, and matching and labelling exercises. With a little thought, all of these can be organised to maximise collaborative activity, and consequently talk. In addition, many of the ideas outlined in Chapter 2 can be usefully adapted to these purposes. For example, students learning about procedural texts might be given two recipes with gaps at the beginning of each step and a list of action processes (or verbs), such as *mix, pour* and *slice*. In pairs they complete both recipes, selecting appropriate processes.

Similarly, cloze exercises where the deletions don't require one correct answer can be completed collaboratively (in pairs or small groups) and shared with the whole class. This allows students to negotiate an appropriate answer and then hear other students' selections and discuss variations in vocabulary choice. The important points to remember are:

- to give students shared responsibilities for completing the task
- to ensure that there's a genuine need to communicate (e.g. a problem to solve or an information gap to fill)
- that students have the background information required to complete the task.

The next stage in the curriculum cycle builds on these understandings in the context of a particular topic or unit of work.

Joint construction

This is the stage at which teachers and students construct a new text based on a shared set of experiences. Note that it has two phases: preparation for joint construction and the construction itself. Some teachers skip over the deconstruction stage and move straight from negotiating the field to preparing for joint construction because students are keen to begin work on the topic. They then go back to deconstruction, in effect making it part of the preparation phase. However, the cycle is fairly flexible, allowing teachers to act on their own judgements about a particular group of students.

Preparation for joint construction is important because it's where students build up the necessary field knowledge. It's also a phase rich in opportunities for process-type talk as students investigate and explore the area, developing vocabulary and grammar specific to the topic and text type. We find them engaged in such activities as guided research, problem-solving tasks, excursions, role plays, interviews and surveys. Which activities are chosen will partly depend on how information is typically organised in a particular text type. For instance, students preparing to write an information report about animals often carry out research guided by a proforma, which might list questions like these:

> *What sort of animal is it?*
>
> *What are its distribution and habitat?*
>
> *What is its diet?*
>
> *What does it look like?*
>
> *How does it reproduce?*

There are a number of ways in which you can encourage talk among students using a proforma — for example, ask them to work in pairs. Alternatively allocate them each a question to research individually and then have them meet with others to combine information and complete a group proforma. The jigsaw technique (Aronson et al. 1977) is a similar means of getting students to talk about research data. Let's look at an example from a unit on Natural Disasters to see how it works.

Initially students were grouped to research particular disasters: one group investigated droughts, another earthquakes, another volcanoes, another cyclones, and so on. The guiding questions for their research were these:

> *Where does this disaster occur?*
>
> *How often does it occur?*
>
> *What causes it?*
>
> *What is its effect?*

When the students had finished their research (which involved reading and taking notes), new groups were formed to include one member from each of the original groups. Thus these new groups contained a drought expert, a volcano expert, a cyclone expert, an earthquake expert, and so on. Students then shared their information and in the process built up considerable group knowledge about a range of natural disasters. Some students of Polynesian descent told traditional tales that accounted for disasters in ways that differed markedly from the explanations found in texts from the school library. Comparing the differences enriched the learning of all the students, giving them a more lively sense of variation in the meanings given to experience.

At this stage in the cycle the teacher has a crucial role in sequencing tasks so that students can develop their understandings of both content and literacy. The notion of talk as a bridge to writing, mentioned earlier, is particularly apposite here. For example, students may well be able to make a telephone from string and cans, but they won't necessarily be able to explain how it works without taking part in a guided discussion about how sound travels (content) — a discussion which also allows for oral rehearsal of an explanation text (literacy).

A sequence of shared activities helps to place all students in a position to contribute ideas and suggestions to the joint construction of a new text. Many *will* contribute, but those who prefer to watch and listen may gain as much, if not more. As the joint text takes shape where everyone can see it, there are wonderful opportunities for showing how spoken language is shaped into written language, and for pointing out features of a particular genre. Whether this is done as a whole class or in smaller groups, the teacher necessarily takes a prominent role (see PEN 96, Imogen Hunt's *Successful Joint Construction*, for a very useful discussion of the kind of teacher talk involved). The completed text can be edited and published in the same way as an individual text; it may even be the object of deconstruction.

Independent construction

Teachers may omit this stage in some units of work, the decision to do so depending on the age of the students and the particular topic and text type. The texts students construct independently may come from the same field as a preceding joint construction or from another, but in either case the text type will be the same and preparation will shadow what they did for joint construction. In other words, it will involve a good deal of process-type talk, especially if students are working in pairs or small groups. Even if they're writing individual texts, they can collaborate in research and preparation for writing. Moreover they may well need their teacher's help (delivered orally) to develop further understandings of grammar by examining effective and ineffective models of the text type, and inevitably they will spend a considerable time negotiating and building up knowledge of the field. Conferencing, editing and publishing their texts will involve still more talk with each other and with their teacher.

It's clear that there are many opportunities for talk during the curriculum cycle. A unit based on the model can incorporate talk about the topic, talk as a bridge between spoken and written language, and talk about text. During the cycle the teacher will sometimes act as coordinator or facilitator, and sometimes adopt a more interventionist role. All this is apparent in the remainder of the chapter, which describes a unit on Simple Machines that followed the cycle. Here you can see how talk was used to develop children's understandings about the topic and to make key points about language use.

Integrating spoken and written language in a unit of work

The unit of work, grounded in Science and Technology, was called Simple Machines. In selecting the topic, the teachers had been led by the children's interests and language needs, and by curriculum demands. The children, who were in two Year 3 classes, were doing some construction work in Creative and Practical Arts and had considered ways of joining and fastening materials. They'd particularly enjoyed simple carpentry and were very interested in tools like the hand drill and the brace and bit. Since the school was undergoing cyclical maintenance at the time, there were plenty of opportunities for them to observe others using tools and simple machines (though not all had equal access to these tools outside school).

The children spoke a range of languages other than English at home, but most were competent users of social English. None the less, like most learners of similar age, they were unfamiliar with the specialised vocabulary of content areas. As a result their teachers tried to program activities based on shared or lived experiences that would encourage them to work in groups and talk with each other about their understandings.

The text type selected for focus was explanation. The children were already familiar with the purposes and features of recounts, narratives, procedures and reports, and were gaining increasingly sophisticated skills in reading and writing this range of texts. To introduce them to this new text type, the teachers decided on asking them to produce explanations of some simple machines in the form of labelled, captioned diagrams. It was thought that this would best prepare them for producing more continuous written explanations about different types of phenomena later on.

Building the field through talk

Initial activities were carefully planned to orientate students to the topic and establish some common understandings for the remainder of the unit. For example, it was decided to consider machines as manufactured objects with more than one moving part.

Predicting

The topic was introduced with the help of a (masked) poster showing a traffic scene — familiar enough to these urban students. As the poster was gradually uncovered, students tried to identify all the machines they could see. This technique, known as visual prediction, encourages students to use some of the vocabulary associated with the topic.

Listing

Next the students worked in pairs to list as many machines as they could think of. When they were unable to name a machine but could describe its appearance and operation, another child or a teacher supplied the name. Then the pairs formed groups of four to combine their lists and consider any further additions. A walk around the school site enabled them to identify further machines in use, and finally a class list of machines was collated.

Categorising

In the following session, the students worked in small groups to divide the machines into categories they devised themselves (e.g. machines used for fun, for work, for learning; indoor and outdoor machines; electric and non-electric). Each group had a photocopy of the class list that they could cut up and reorganise. This activity placed considerable demands on their language for negotiation, as well as their command of vocabulary associated with the topic.

Justifying

Once they were satisfied with their categories, the groups presented and explained them to the rest of the class, who had to listen carefully in order to question them. Sometimes students referred to their own group's choices to challenge particular decisions. Presentation introduced an element of performance talk, and the negotiation of categories with a considerably larger group put additional demands on students' vocabulary and social skills.

Extending understandings

Several machines (initially a CD player, computer and car) were selected for consideration. Four questions were set out at the top of a large matrix, and simple responses were worked out and entered during a whole class discussion (see Fig. 10.2).

Students were then given a proforma incorporating these questions to guide them in researching other machines (e.g. a camera, a flushing toilet and a refrigerator). Working in pairs, they were encouraged not only to use a range of printed sources but to supplement them by questioning adults at

Name of machine	Why was it invented?	What did it replace?	What is it made of?	How does it work?
CD player	to play music to get a good sound	record players	metal, plastic	a laser beam reads a pattern of pits and flats on the underneath of the CD and the machine changes it into vibrations
car	to move people around	horses buggies bicycles	metal, plastic glass, fabric	a petrol-driven motor makes the wheels go round; the steering wheel helps control the wheels
computer	to process and store information	filing cabinets typists	plastic, metal	we make little electric currents when we type on the keyboard and these flow through the microchips

FIG. 10.2. A MATRIX FOR DESCRIBING MACHINES

home or others involved in jobs which used these machines. They added their results to the class matrix as they completed their research.

Of course this kind of matrix provides a means of organising and storing information, but it can also be used to generate spoken language:

T: Paul, using the matrix, please tell me about CD players.

P: Uh, a CD player was invented to play music that sounds good. It replaced records which used to get scratched and are too big. Uh, a CD player is made from metal and plastic. It works by having a disc with lots of tiny pits and flats on the underneath and a laser beam um . . .

T: Yes, a laser beam reads . . .

P: A laser beam reads these pits and flats and the machine makes them into vibrations. That's what sound is.

T: Good. Now you choose someone else and a machine for them to talk about.

P: Sarina, would you please tell the class about computers?

When the matrix had a good many entries, the teachers posed some different kinds of questions, such as *What have these machines meant to people?*

Two students explore how a hand drill works. At this stage talk will include a lot of referential language; technical terms will come more easily later.

How have lives changed? Whose lives are easier? What did this mean for people's jobs? Students discussed some of the complex issues surrounding technological change — for example, balancing convenience on the one hand against job losses on the other.

Since the teachers had decided that this unit would shape the term's programs, the students were also engaged in reading related factual texts like *The Paper Skyscraper* and *What Shall I Use?* (Drew 1992). In their library work they had encountered a number of different types of explanation texts, where the teachers were able to point out the use of diagrams, labels and captions. Nevertheless these texts caused a certain amount of difficulty for many of the students, and so reading groups were organised around suitable texts about robotics and machines for specific purposes. Students worked through exercises for comprehension and word study, including sequencing information, locating key words in text and diagrams, dictionary work and word building. Spelling activities during the unit were also related to machines.

An excursion to a technology museum was aimed at developing students' understanding of the social impact of technology. They looked at exhibits of domestic life at different times and considered the ways in which people responded to particular needs and environments. The information texts on display beside exhibits also provided models of explanatory texts in use. After the excursion they recounted significant events of the day as a whole class and then wrote individual recounts in a letter home. As teachers talked with individual students during the writing process, they were able to provide a good deal of support and direction about the ways texts work. They also had a chance to gauge the extent to which students understood the relationship between inventions and people's changing lifestyles.

It's clear that introducing a topic and extending students' understandings of it offers numerous opportunities for them to talk. Often these students were working collaboratively with minimal direction because of the way an activity was designed or because they could rely on a worksheet or proforma (e.g. in listing, categorising or researching). At other times the teachers provided quite explicit direction and guidance by questioning, prompting and making teaching points (e.g. when discussing the effects of technology or pointing out features of texts).

Deconstruction
Developing literacy through talk
As well as negotiating the topic of machines, the teachers opened up the field of literacy by reviewing text types. Students worked in small groups to identify the purposes and features of a given collection of texts, which served to focus their attention on language and made them review some of the understandings about text and context they'd previously developed. Then they looked at a number of explanatory texts (e.g. junior encyclopedias, pamphlets on tooth decay, posters of suburban water and sewerage systems) and discussed:

- the topic
- the intended audience
- features such as titles, diagrams, labels and captions.

Next they compared explanations with other text types they were familiar with and came up with some ideas about particular language features. For example, they pointed to the presence of people in narratives (individual participants) and their absence in explanations (which have generic participants). They considered the effectiveness and accessibility of each text, suggesting that some of the everyday texts would have been more successful if they'd been accompanied by diagrams. They also observed something of the importance of background knowledge, commenting that some texts were difficult to understand because they 'didn't know anything about that thing'.

This phase led on to preparing for a jointly constructed text. The students spent some time looking at a bicycle that had been brought in. One class did this together, but the other class did it in small groups. The groups allowed for a good deal more participation, though some students struggled for terms like *brake* and *tyre*. Each group was given a diagram of the bike marked with arrows and had to provide names for the indicated parts and describe their function (e.g. *the rider sits on the seat; the handlebars allow the rider to steer the bike; the brakes stop the wheels turning*). Then all the groups came together and jointly constructed labels and captions for a class version of their worksheets. Finally they developed an oral explanation of the text, using the labels and captions as a prompt.

The bicycle had proved a challenging subject for explanation, and talk moved easily to the idea of some machines being more complex than others. Teachers and students decided that for their purposes simple machines were those without motors. Although this wasn't a scientifically accurate definition, it suited the purpose of the unit because machines without motors were the safest to study.

The students then moved to considering small hand-held machines which had an observable sequence of actions. An egg beater was selected as the focus for a jointly constructed text.

Joint construction

In preparing for joint construction, small groups of students handled egg beaters and shared what they knew about them. They were asked to talk about what each part did and how the parts worked together to make the whole machine work. Naturally there was a good deal of language generated as students negotiated roles, commented on their observations of the beater, posed explanations and clarified others' suggestions. Each group chose a member to share their oral explanation with the whole class, using a beater to demonstrate. Then teachers and students decided on common terms for the parts of the beater and jointly constructed labels and captions to describe each part's function (see Fig. 10.3). The text of the captions was essentially the oral explanation sequence.

Individual construction

The jointly constructed diagram provided a blueprint for individuals to prepare a similar diagram with an oral explanation to accompany it. In pairs, students selected simple machines like kitchen tongs, a stapler, an in-line skate, a garlic crusher, a hand drill and an umbrella. The teachers found

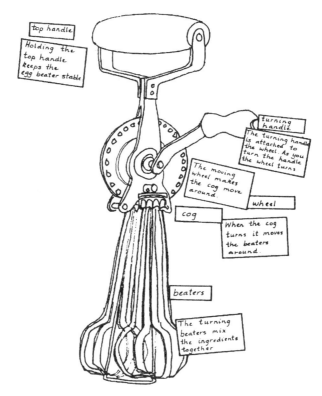

top handle

Holding the
top handle
keeps the
egg beater stable

turning
handle

The turning handle
is attached to
the wheel. As you
turn the handle
the wheel turns

The moving
wheel makes
the cog move
around

wheel

cog

When the cog
turns it moves
the beaters
around.

beaters

The turning
beaters mix
the ingredients
together

FIG. 10.3. A JOINTLY CONSTRUCTED DIAGRAM OF AN EGG BEATER

they needed a good deal of help in naming parts (e.g. the *lock* on the tongs, the *struts* on the umbrella) and in talking through their explanation sequences (e.g. *When I push the button of the umbrella up the stem, the struts straighten and the fabric unfolds. When the button is locked, the fabric is tight and keeps out the rain*). Each pair of students then joined another pair and they shared their explanations. Having an audience helped them move along the mode continuum towards written-like texts: they had to be more concise and clear and name parts rather than using *it, this* and *here.*

Next the students constructed their individual texts — that is, they drew a simple machine and drafted labels and captions based on their previous work. The drafts were conferenced with the teachers and other students, and the teachers also heard the oral explanations. Fig. 10.4 shows one of the students' published texts.

Coda

The final task in the unit asked students to take the sorts of understandings and associated language they had been building up and apply them to solve an imaginary problem. After a prolonged period of rain, they were well

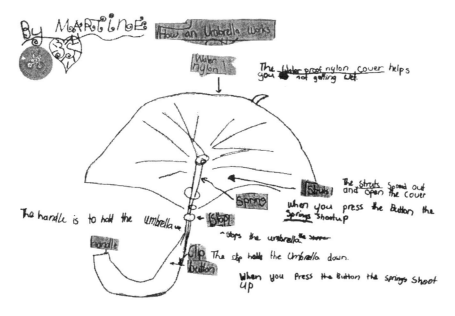

FIG. 10.4. EXPLANATORY DIAGRAM OF AN UMBRELLA BY MARTINE (9)

aware of the difficulties of communicating decisions about wet weather playground arrangements across a busy school on a large site. Accordingly they were given this design brief:

Design a simple machine that enables a decision about wet weather playground duties to be quickly communicated to all the teachers in the school. The machine should be easy to operate and not too costly. Your group will present the design to the class as a large labelled captioned diagram which they will explain.

The task was undertaken with a good deal of enthusiasm and certainly generated a lot of talk. Teachers could constantly hear the language of suggestion (*Let's have a . . . Yes, what about . . ? No, we can't do that . . . I know, why don't we . . ?*). The groups worked very well together and, not surprisingly, the responses to such an open-ended brief were very different. However, presenting the designs to the class disclosed a need for a good deal more modelling and rehearsal to make the explanations self-sufficient, as the following example demonstrates:

There's a bell on the top to tell Ms Treloar to pull the string. And then it tells all the teachers that it's raining and to stay inside. And the bottom bell just not far away from the other one tells you that you can go outside — it's all right to go outside.

Largely unplanned observational assessment took place throughout the unit, and formal assessment tasks, using criteria related to teaching/learning outcomes, were built in at different points. The students used the design brief for peer assessment in the final task, and they were also asked to reflect on their group work skills. In both cases they relied mainly on spoken language.

Conclusion

Spoken language is clearly an integral part of any literacy program. Hands-on interactive tasks are useful for orientating students to topics and may well be more motivating than other types of task. However, without adequate support, students can still be left stranded at commonsense understandings. To develop more abstract understandings, teachers have to carefully stage teaching and learning and vary the degree of control they have over lesson content. There will be times when they need to make teaching points and times when students work together with minimal direction. But at all times talk will be the medium through which conceptual and linguistic understandings are constructed. Talking among themselves and with their teachers is a vital element in the move students must make from familiar, context-bound observations to the more academic, written-like understandings inherent in curriculum areas.

Acknowledgement

The Simple Machines unit was developed with Stephanie Searle and Tracey Thollar at Belmore South Public School. We were fortunate to have access to the resources of the Metropolitan East Disadvantaged Schools Program, and particularly to the expertise of Katina Zammit, the literacy consultant.

References

Aronson, E., Blaney, N., Stephan, C., Sides, J. & Snapp, M. 1977, *The Jigsaw Classroom*, Sage Publications, Beverly Hills, CA.

Bartlett, F. 1932, *Remembering*, Cambridge University Press, Cambridge.

Board of Studies New South Wales 1994, *Otitis Media and Aboriginal Children: A Handbook for Teachers and Communities*, Board of Studies NSW, Sydney.

—— 1996, *A Guide to the English K–6 Syllabus and Support Document*, New South Wales Department of School Education, Sydney.

Bremner, S. 1995, Teaching English in the Key Learning Area of English, Paper presented to the English as a Second Language Retraining Course, New South Wales Department of School Education, Sydney.

Brown, G. & Yule, G. 1983, *Teaching the Spoken Language*, Cambridge University Press, Cambridge.

Bruner, J. 1986, *Actual Minds, Possible Worlds*, Harvard University Press, New York.

Christie, F. 1985, *Language Education*, Deakin University Press, Geelong.

Collins, J. & Michaels, S. 1986, 'Speaking and writing: discourse strategies and the acquisition of literacy', in J. Cook-Gumperz (ed.), *The Social Construction of Literacy*, Cambridge University Press, London.

Connelly, F. & Clandinin, J. 1990, 'Stories of experience and narrative enquiry', *Educational Researcher*, vol. 19, no. 5, pp. 2–14.

Cummins, J. 1979, 'Linguistic interdependence and the educational development of bilingual children', *Review of Educational Research*, no. 49, pp. 221–51.

—— & Swain, M. 1986, *Bilingalism in Education*, Longman, London.

Curriculum Corporation 1994, *A Statement on English for Australian Schools*, a joint project of the States, Territories and the Commonwealth of Australia initiated by the Australian Education Council, Curriculum Corporation, Melbourne.

Cusworth, R. 1994, 'Newstime in junior primary classrooms: quality oral narrative or technical routine?', in G. Halliwell (ed.), *Early Childhood Perspectives on Assessment, Justice and Quality*, Australian Curriculum Studies Association, Canberra.

—— 1995, 'Newstime in early childhood classrooms: intention vs reality', *Research in Australian Early Childhood Education*, vol. 2, no. 1, pp. 51–60.

de Bono, E. 1987, *Six Thinking Hats*, Penguin, London.

Department of Employment, Education and Training 1995, *Langwij Comes to School*, DEET, Canberra.

Derewianka, B. 1990, *Exploring How Texts Work*, Primary English Teaching Association, Sydney.

Drew, D. 1992, *What Should I Use?* and *The Paper Skyscraper*, Rigby Realization and Technology Series, Rigby Heinemann, Melbourne.

Eades, D. 1993, *Aboriginal English*, PEN 93, Primary English Teaching Association, Sydney.

—— 1995, *Aboriginal English*, Aboriginal Literacy Resource Kit, Aboriginal Curriculum Unit, Board of Studies New South Wales, Sydney.

Education Department of South Australia 1990, *ESL Student Needs Assessment Procedures R–10*, Education Department of SA, Adelaide.

—— 1990, *Oral Communication in English*, Education Department of SA, Adelaide.

Egan, F. 1991, 'Learning through language', in F. McKay (ed.), *Public and Private Lessons: The Language of Teaching and Learning*, Australian Reading Association, Melbourne.

Evans, J. 1994, *Oral Language: The Developmental Continuum*, Longman Cheshire, Melbourne (originally developed as *First Steps* by the Education Department of Western Australia).

Evans, M. 1984, 'Play beyond play: its role in formal informative speech', in L. Galda & A. Pelligrini (eds), *Play Language and Stories*, Ablex, New Jersey.

Fox, C. 1988, 'Poppies will make them grant', in M. Meek & C. Mills (eds), *Language and Literacy in the Primary School*, Falmer Press, London.

—— 1993, *At the Very Edge of the Forest*, Cassell, London.

Gallas, K. 1992, 'When the children take the chair: a study of sharing time in a primary classroom', *Language Arts*, vol. 69, pp. 172–82.

Gibbons, P. 1991, *Learning to Learn in a Second Language*, Primary English Teaching Association, Sydney.

—— 1992, 'Supporting bilingual students for success', *Australian Journal of Language and Literacy*, vol. 15, no. 3, pp. 225–36.

—— 1993, 'Talk: a bridge to literacy in the classroom', *TESOL in Context*, vol. 3, no. 1, pp. 32–34.

Halliday, M. A. K. 1985, *Spoken and Written Language*, Deakin University Press, Geelong.

—— 1994, 'A language development approach to education', in N. Bird et al., *Language and Learning*, Institute of Language in Education, Hong Kong Education Department, Hong Kong.

Hammond, J. 1992, 'Spoken and written language: implications for language and literacy development', English Literacy Round Table Papers, Board of Studies New South Wales, Sydney.

Hardy, B. 1975, *Tellers and Listeners*, Athlone Press, London.

Heath, S. B. 1982, 'What no bedtime story means: narrative skills at home and school', *Language in Society*, vol. 11, pp. 49–76.

—— 1983, *Ways with Words*, Cambridge University Press, Cambridge.

Hill, S. 1992, *Games That Work: Co-operative Games and Activities for the Primary School Classroom*, Eleanor Curtain, Melbourne.

Hunt, I. 1994, *Successful Joint Construction*, PEN 96, Primary English Teaching Association, Sydney.

Jones, P. 1993, Spoken language and genre-based pedagogy: a case study, MA (TESOL) thesis, University of Technology, Sydney.

Kamler, B. 1994, Morning talk as a gendered language practice, Paper presented at the AARE Conference, University of Newcastle, Newcastle, November.

Labov, W. 1972, 'The logic of non-standard English', in W. Labov, *Language in the Inner City: Studies in the Black English Vernacular*, University of Pennsylvania Press, Philadelphia.

Martin, J. R. 1985, 'Language, register and genre', in F. Christie (ed.), *Children Writing Course Reader*, Deakin University Press, Geelong.

—— 1989, 'Technicality and abstraction: language for the creation of specialised texts', in F. Christie (ed.), *Writing in Schools: A Reader*, Deakin University Press, Geelong.

—— & Rothery, J. 1982, *Writing Project Report*, Working Papers in Linguistics No. 2, Department of Linguistics, University of Sydney, Sydney.

McGregor, R. & Meirs, M. 1987, *Talking and Listening K–12: A Guide to Assessment and Reporting*, The English Club, n.p.

Meek, M. 1988, *How Texts Teach What Readers Learn*, Thimble Press, Stroud, Glos.

—— 1991, *On Being Literate*, Bodley Head, London.

—— & Mills, C. (eds) 1988, *Language and Literacy in the Primary School*, Falmer Press, London.

Metropolitan East Disadvantaged Schools Program 1991, *The Recount Genre*, New South Wales Department of Education, Sydney.

—— 1992, *Animals: The Action Pack*, Metropolitan East Disadvantaged Schools Program, Sydney.

Nation, I. S. P. & Thomas, G. I. 1988, *Communication Activities*, Occasional Paper No. 13, English Language Institute, Victoria University of Wellington, Wellington.

New South Wales Department of Education n.d., *Information Skills in the School*, NSW Department of Education, Sydney.

New South Wales Department of School Education 1990, *Aboriginal Reflections from ELIC*, NSW Department of School Education, Sydney.

Ontario Ministry of Education 1987, 'Language aloud allowed . . . even encouraged', draft support document in I. Pringle & J. Fox, *The Assessment of Oral English Draft Paper*, Centre for Applied Language Studies, Carleton University, Ottawa.

Painter, C. 1985, *Learning the Mother Tongue*, Deakin University Press, Geelong.

—— 1986, 'The role of interaction in learning to speak and learning to write', in C. Painter & J. R. Martin (eds), *Writing to Mean: Teaching Genres across the Curriculum*, Occasional Papers No. 9, Applied Linguistics Association of Australia, n.p.

Spender, D. 1990, *Man Made Language*, Routledge, London.

Unsworth, L. (ed.) 1993, *Literacy Learning and Teaching: Language as Social Practice in the Primary School*, Macmillan, Melbourne.

Widdowson, H. G. 1983, *Learning Purpose and Language Use*, Oxford University Press, Oxford.

Young, R. 1991, *Critical Theory and Classroom Talk*, Multilingual Matters, Cleverdon, Philadelphia.

Notes on contributors

Penni Brydon has taught K–6 in both urban and rural schools, as well as adult literacy at TAFE. She is the Aboriginal Education Resource Teacher (K–2) at Dubbo West Public School, and is currently training as a Reading Recovery teacher.

Kathy Cree and **Sandra Donaldson** have taught in disadvantaged schools for many years. Both try to provide students with the skills to become 'active' learners, taking on roles and responsibilities to solve problems and complete design tasks whenever the opportunities present themselves.

Robyn Cusworth is Co-Director of the Master of Teaching degree in the Education Faculty at the University of Sydney, where she lectures in curriculum, literacy and drama. She is an experienced teacher who enjoys working collaboratively with other teachers interested in changing or developing their practice. Her PhD explored newstime as a curriculum phenomenon in K–2 classrooms.

Isobel Kirk has expanded on a successful acting career to become one of Australia's foremost voice and performance specialists. Recently she convened an international symposium, 'The Art and Science of Voice', at the National Institute of Dramatic Art, where she was Head of Voice Studies for four years. She is a founding board member of the Australian Voice Association.

Lesley Mills is an Aboriginal Education Resource Teacher in the North Coast region of New South Wales. As well as presenting workshops on Aboriginal literacy and learning styles, she has prepared resources recognised by the Board of Studies and the Curriculum Corporation.

Vicki Pogulis has been teaching in urban and rural primary schools for twenty-five years and has also had experience as an adult TESOL teacher. She is currently Executive Teacher (Acting) at Glebe Public School and will be Executive Teacher at Ultimo Public School in 1997.

Victoria Roberts and **Vivienne Nicoll** have between them amassed over forty years' experience in primary teaching, teacher-librarianship, literacy consultancy, professional development and university lecturing. Both have published on various aspects of literacy teaching, especially children's literature. Currently Victoria is a teacher-librarian and Vivienne is PETA's Acquisitions Editor.

Kathleen Rushton works as a teacher of English to adult migrants and as an ESL teacher at Redfern Primary School. Her main interest is developing literacy with students who speak non-standard varieties of English.

Tina Sharpe is an independent literacy and learning consultant, writing curriculum materials and presenting at staff development days. She worked for seven years as a consultant with the Catholic Education Office, Sydney, and current lectures part-time on TESOL and the NSW K–6 English Syllabus at three Sydney universities.